# ADULT LIFE SKILLS FOR OLDER TEENS

LEARN TO COOK, MAINTAIN A HOME, AND EVERYTHING YOU NEED TO KNOW ABOUT RENTING, FORMING HEALTHY RELATIONSHIPS, AND KNOWING YOUR WORTH. (VOL. 1)

HOME EDITION

KATIE WEBSDELL

© **Copyright 2022 - All rights reserved.**

The content contained within this book may not be reproduced, duplicated or transmitted without direct written permission from the author or the publisher.

Under no circumstances will any blame or legal responsibility be held against the publisher, or author, for any damages, reparation, or monetary loss due to the information contained within this book, either directly or indirectly.

**Legal Notice:**

This book is copyright protected. It is only for personal use. You cannot amend, distribute, sell, use, quote or paraphrase any part, or the content within this book, without the consent of the author or publisher.

**Disclaimer Notice:**

Please note the information contained within this document is for educational and entertainment purposes only. All effort has been executed to present accurate, up to date, reliable, and complete information. No warranties of any kind are declared or implied. Readers acknowledge that the author is not engaged in the rendering of legal, financial, medical or professional advice. The content within this book has been derived from various sources. Please consult a licensed professional before attempting any techniques outlined in this book.

By reading this document, the reader agrees that under no circumstances is the author responsible for any losses, direct or indirect, that are incurred as a result of the use of the information contained within this document, including, but not limited to, errors, omissions, or inaccuracies.

# CONTENTS

| | |
|---|---|
| *Introduction: Adulting 101* | vii |
| 1. THE KITCHEN IS THE HEART OF THE HOME | 1 |
| Essential Kitchen Tools | 3 |
| Cookware | 3 |
| Utensils | 5 |
| Dishes and Other Gadgets | 10 |
| Knife Skills | 13 |
| Standard Measures in Cooking | 17 |
| Cooking Temperatures | 19 |
| Basic Cooking Terms | 20 |
| Vitamins and Minerals | 24 |
| Protein, Carbs, and Fats | 27 |
| Meal Time Ideas | 29 |
| Lunch Or Dinner | 37 |
| Food Preservation | 41 |
| Shopping Tips | 42 |
| Water Intake | 46 |
| 2. KEEPING YOUR HOME CLEAN—THE TOOLS YOU NEED AND HOW TO USE THEM | 48 |
| What to Give, What to Keep | 50 |
| Cleaning the House | 54 |
| The Benefits of Cleaning | 56 |
| How to Clean Your Space | 59 |
| The Toilet | 62 |
| The Shower Head | 65 |
| Cleaning the Oven | 66 |
| Cleaning the Refrigerator | 68 |
| Laundry | 69 |

3. ESSENTIAL HOME MAINTENANCE, CHECKS, AND SECURITY ENHANCEMENTS — 80
   When to Inspect Your Home — 81
   Boiler Maintenance Checks — 82
   Gutters — 83
   Air Vents — 84
   Radiators — 86
   Drains — 87
   Turning Off Your Water Supply — 89
   Tripped Circuit Breaker — 90
   Hanging a Picture — 91
   How To Put Up a Shelf — 93
   Patching a Hole — 94
   Squeaky Hinges — 96
   Lost Keys — 96
   Keeping Documents Safe — 98
   Cyber and Physical Security — 99

4. ESSENTIAL INFO YOU NEED FOR RENTING — 105
   Plan Your Budget — 106
   Make a Criteria — 107
   You and Your Landlord — 108
   Extending or Ending Lease/Tenancy — 109
   Documents to Keep — 110
   The Cost of Renting — 110
   Cost Saving Strategies — 117

5. PERSONAL CARE—TAKING CARE OF YOUR HAIR, SKIN, AND BODY — 119
   Skin Care — 119
   Hair Care — 122
   Dental Hygiene — 124
   Body Hygiene — 126
   Shaving — 127
   Physical Fitness and Health — 127

| | |
|---|---|
| Healthy Sleeping | 131 |
| Dress to Impress | 132 |
| Purchasing Clothes | 133 |
| 6. HEALTH INSURANCE AND FIRST AID KNOW-HOWS | 136 |
| Filling in Forms | 136 |
| Medical Insurance | 137 |
| Dental Insurance | 140 |
| Emergency Contacts | 142 |
| First Aid | 142 |
| 7. FORMING SAFE AND HEALTHY RELATIONSHIPS | 148 |
| Romantic Relationships | 148 |
| Sex and Relationships | 151 |
| Online Dating | 152 |
| Making Friends | 153 |
| 8. KNOWING YOUR WORTH AND BEING POSITIVE | 154 |
| Emotional Intelligence | 155 |
| Dealing With Emotions | 156 |
| Know Your Manners | 157 |
| Etiquette | 157 |
| Staying Positive | 159 |
| Loving-Kindness Meditation | 159 |
| Think of the Best Version of Yourself | 160 |
| Get Rid of Negativity | 160 |
| Remove Toxic Friends | 161 |
| Celebrate Your Accomplishments | 161 |
| Asking for Help | 162 |
| Know Your Self-Worth | 163 |
| *Afterword* | 167 |
| *Also by Katie Websdell* | 169 |
| *Bibliography* | 171 |

# INTRODUCTION: ADULTING 101

Time goes by so slowly when you're a child, and then, as an adult, it goes by in the blink of an eye.

— DAVID LOWERY

I was so excited to grow up! Like you, I couldn't wait to be an independent version of myself, in control of every aspect of my own life, a fully functioning member of society. I was elated. But when I reached adulthood, it looked more like a desert island than the tropical island I was hoping for.

How often has a grown-up got in the way of your plans or stopped you from doing something you really wanted to do? How often have you been frustrated when they told you that you'd thank them for it one day? Well, maybe this book can shed light on why they stopped us from doing what we wanted, and perhaps we may thank those adults later in our lives.

With all my excitement about adulthood and independence, my vision became tunneled, focusing only on what I was excited to do and not on the responsibility of being independent. This is the thing that I think a lot of teenagers and young adults face. They are blinded by the glitz and the glamor of the adult lifestyle while often forgetting the reality.

And honestly, who could blame us? Somehow, milk was always in the fridge when I made my cereal (someone remembered to buy it). I rarely considered what food cost and never needed to pay any bills. (Utilities? What's that?).

So when I ventured out into the world by myself, I realized that the world, freedom, and my own rules, were not all I thought they would be. It was a rude awakening, and there was no manager I could speak to about canceling my subscription to adulthood.

I had to make my own rules and was wildly ill-equipped to make them. Who thought it would be safe to put me in charge? Standing alone in my apartment,

INTRODUCTION: ADULTING 101 | ix

struggling to understand the utility bill in my hand, I realized how much was expected of me.

I never called home with questions about things that were stressors for me. I wanted to stand on my own two feet and work it out, even if something was tricky to understand.

Living on my own did bring freedom, but adulting is so exhausting that I didn't even want to use this newfound freedom.

Staying home and watching TV with family was a young teen's punishment on a Friday night. Especially when there was only one TV set in the whole house! Yes, that's how old I am! But that turned out to be my greatest luxury as an adult.

But this was just one aspect of the drastic change that I had to face. Suddenly, I was without my family, childhood friends, and all the people I greatly depended on. I had to figure out how and where to do my laundry. I had to either buy or make my own food. I would even have to keep my little apartment clean and tidy without my family chasing after me to do it. The hardest part was that I had to learn how to budget. Not just for the week but for the coming months.

I learned how to do all of it, little by little. I made many stupid mistakes, more than I care to admit, and it wasn't until I reached my early 20s that I felt like a qualified adult.

Maybe you haven't given too much thought to adulting. It feels like it's far away. You're still in high school or college, having the time of your life. Your life at present probably revolves around studies, friends, and occasional romantic relationships. Or perhaps you are beginning to think about life outside of college, what you will do, where you will live, and how it will all work, which is normal too. I get it. Your teens and early 20s are all about discovering who you really are. Still, you often don't discover who you are until you discover your independence.

You may not realize that adulthood is right around the corner, and you're probably not prepared for it. The school doesn't teach you how to look after a home, budget, or know your worth. And our parents and family members don't or can't always teach us these valuable life skills either. This is not because they are being malicious or setting us up for failure; it's just that once they have learned these skills, it becomes almost second nature to them. They may have forgotten that there was a time when they didn't know certain things and that now you need to know them too. Let's be honest some things you don't want to learn from your parents. So treat this book as an independent source of knowledge.

## WHO AM I?

So now that you're here with this guide in hand, you're probably wondering who is the genius that decided to write this book. My name is Katie Websdell, and I am a mom of three beautiful kids. Watching my children grow—quite rapidly, I might add, I realized that they are very likely to fall into the trap of unpreparedness I once fell into. Realizing they won't be the only ones to fall into this trap, I decided to start writing this book. I have watched myself, my younger siblings, and countless others go through the same thing, and I have decided to stop the cycle.

I am genuinely passionate about helping young people like you take their first steps into the world while feeling prepared. I want you to feel confident when you leave the safety and security of your home.

I left school at the tender age of 16 and bounced between academic prospects. While I didn't attend college in the traditional sense, I was tossed into adulthood at a very young age and had to find my feet quickly.

I learned a lot of experiences in what seems like a short space of time, but not without a bit of fumbling and stumbling. I decided that no one should face the anxiety-inducing uncertainty I encountered at such a young age. That has been my motivation to write this book.

## WHAT IS THIS BOOK ABOUT?

I've written this 'Home Edition' book to share vital knowledge. I want you to feel ready for just about anything that you might encounter. Granted, you won't be prepared for everything. That would mean being able to see the future, and there is no fun in that. But the best time to learn and begin equipping yourself with adult life skills is right now!

As you know, school doesn't teach you the practical aspects of being an adult. Going through these experiences alone can sometimes be overwhelming. Even now, at my age, I sometimes feel that I have no idea what I'm doing! Becoming an adult is a big step, and I want to make it as easy for you as possible.

We'll be covering several topics. We're going to start off in the kitchen. You might have some experience in the kitchen, maybe frying an egg or making an omelet, but we're going to expand on it. We're not just going to look at cooking but also buying groceries, how to keep your food fresh, and what a healthy meal should look like.

Keeping your home clean and tidy may sound boring and not on your priority list. Still, it is crucial for your physical health and safety and your emotional and mental well-being. Nothing is quite as comforting as returning to a clean and tidy home! We'll look at how to declutter your space, what products and tools you'll need to clean, and we'll also look at how to do laundry.

Feeling safe and secure at home can make or break your first experience of living alone. It's not something we think about very often. I always assumed that my home was safe until I experienced a break-in. Luckily, there are things that you can do to make sure that you are always safe.

Keeping your home in great shape can be a never-ending story. You may have seen family members working on small projects around the house, like cleaning out gutters, patching up holes in walls, or fixing squeaky hinges. You'll get a crash course on doing all this, so your home always looks great.

Cyber security wasn't a big thing when I was venturing into the world. These days, it's an extra detail we need to take care of. Imagine logging into your banking account only to find that someone has made extravagant purchases using your money! We're going to look at how to keep all your digital information safe from cyber criminals, from your Wi-Fi, passwords, and being able to back up your data.

You'll probably need to rent a place to live sooner than you think. When I rented my first apartment, I was shocked at all the extra costs. I also didn't realize that it's not just rent that you must pay, but utilities like water and electricity, and other costs such as rates and insurance! We'll look at all that to ensure you can find an affordable dream apartment.

When we look good, we feel good. It's science! We will discuss personal hygiene, exercise, sleep, and wardrobe. All these things will leave you looking and feeling like you can conquer the world!

Here's something I didn't know until I was in my 30s: Health insurance is super important, especially if you live in the US! When you start researching health insurance, your mind will spin with all the different options available. We'll break them down in the health insurance chapter to make it easier.

What happens when you hurt yourself at home while doing some DIY? Knowing some basic first aid can sometimes save you from an unnecessary trip to the emergency room. Minor bumps, cuts, and scrapes can be treated at home. We'll also look at how to treat the common cold with over-the-counter medications.

Dating and relationships change as you become an adult, especially when you're alone. When you find yourself in a new city, you will need to make friends, which can be a daunting experience. We'll look at what you can do to make new friends and how to stay safe on dating apps.

When I first moved out, my emotions were all over the place. I was happy, sad, excited, nervous, and scared. It was sobering and sometimes overwhelming, doing things on my own, running out of money, and not feeling like I had control of my finances. I was proud and didn't want to ask for help, even though I needed it. We're going to dedicate a chapter to our emotions. We will try to understand them, acknowledge them, and deal with them.

## GET READY FOR YOUR ADULTING CRASH COURSE!

What you just read may sound like a lot. You're probably already overwhelmed. I get it! Realizing that all these things are just around the corner is a huge step!

Remember that you're not alone in this. You have this book to guide you as you take your first steps into the world of adulthood. Everything is going to be okay; I promise!

So, let's get started and see how you can begin building a happy, healthy, and successful life.

# 1

## THE KITCHEN IS THE HEART OF THE HOME

Whenever I think back to my childhood home, being with family, I always looked forward to a delicious home-cooked meal, especially Sunday dinner. I want to say the whole family helped, but the real magic came from my mom and grandma.

When I first began living independently, I survived on tinned hot dogs, instant mashed potato, coffee, and whatever junk food I could afford. Needless to say, I quickly realized that this was not healthy, and I had to figure out how to make my own healthy meals. Also, no one warns you that the cost of buying fast food can quickly add up and can take a hefty chunk out of your budget.

When cooking for yourself for the first time, your meals don't have to be gourmet works of art. If they are nutritious and easy enough for you to make yourself, you're on the right path! As you become more experienced in the kitchen, you'll be able to experiment a little more.

You need to know essential things, like basic cooking terminology, temperatures, and measurements. You also need to understand what nutrients, vitamins, and minerals you'll need to keep yourself healthy. I'll also be sharing some of my favorite breakfast, lunch, and dinner recipes for you to try. Don't worry; these recipes are super simple!

There are also some things that you need to know about going grocery shopping. I have hacks for saving time and money with the simple trick of grocery shopping based on a menu I have set for the month. This means I never have to wonder what to cook. It helps me avoid adding unnecessary items to my shopping cart (trolly). You also need to ensure that you read food labels and know what "best before" and "use by" dates are all about.

We'll also look at how food should be stored to help keep it fresh for longer and lessen the likelihood of food poisoning. Last but not least, I'll show you ways in which you can save some money by growing vegetables and herbs on your windowsill!

## ESSENTIAL KITCHEN TOOLS

My very first kitchen was bare. I didn't know what I needed. I only had a cutlery set, some plates, a few mugs, and some baking dishes donated mainly by my family to get me started. So few items made cooking something as simple as scrambled eggs challenging. The right tools for the job will make your cooking experience much easier!

It can get quite expensive to go out and buy all these items at once, but start small and work your way up until you have a fully equipped kitchen. Remember, Rome wasn't built in a day!

### COOKWARE

Pots, pans, and everything else—that's what cookware is. You'll need a few essential pieces to be able to prepare some delicious meals for yourself. If you can get the better quality ones, they last much longer!

**Non-Stick Frying Pan**

Essential for making my favorite go-to quick meal of scrambled eggs!

The non-stick surface helps a lot when washing up too. You can also use the pan for other dishes, like searing meat and making sauces. Many stores sell a combo pack of these frying pans, which lets you have two or three different sizes. It's vital to get the proper utensils for non-stick cookware; it stops them from getting scratched. If they get scratched, the food sticks and burns, and you don't want that.

**Saucepan**

A saucepan is great for cooking pasta and boiling potatoes or vegetables.

I would recommend getting a medium-sized saucepan to start. You can see if you should add a bigger or smaller saucepan to your collection, depending on how many people you are cooking for.

**Stock Pot**

If you love soups or stews, you'll need a stock pot. Think of a stock pot as a jumbo saucepan! You'll be able to make considerable amounts of soup, which you can freeze and save for later, saving you money too!

## Sheet Pans

Sheet pans, also known as baking trays, can be used to make various delicious foods. You can bake cookies and roast vegetables and meat. Tip: Place a sheet of baking paper or aluminum foil on the tray before adding your food. It will need minimum cleaning afterward!

## Glass Baking Dishes

These are perfect for making casseroles in the oven. They're also microwave-friendly, so you can use them to heat up or thoroughly cook food in the microwave.

## UTENSILS

This broad term covers all the tools you need for cutting, slicing, stirring, and measuring. Examples include; a ladle, balloon whisk, peeler, tongs, wooden spoon, and spatulas.

## Knives

There's nothing more frustrating than wanting to cut something and not having the right knife for it! A complete knife set can have up to 18 knives and be quite expensive. The first knife you should get is a chef's knife. You'll be able to use it for just about everything!

BONING

MEAT CLEAVER

CHEF'S

FORK

CARVING

BREAD

STEAK

SMALL BREAD

PARING

When expanding your knife collection, I suggest getting a serrated knife and a paring knife. A serrated knife helps to cut loaves of bread and soft vegetables easily. In contrast, a paring knife is excellent for slicing small, delicate vegetables. Tip: Invest in a knife sharpener, especially for your chef's and paring knife. A sharp knife is a joy to use. It saves you lots of time and makes you look like a pro once you have mastered those chopping skills!

## Measuring Spoons

Some recipes, especially those for baked goods, need exact measurements, so it's always great to have a set of measuring spoons. You will see these in recipes asking for a teaspoon (tsp) or a tablespoon (tbsp) measure. These will be super handy when you're first starting out and aren't sure about your measurements. After a while, you might be able to measure it by "eyeballing" it!

## Measuring Cups

Measuring cups will help you to measure larger quantities in cooking and baking. A recipe may ask for a cup full of an ingredient such as sugar or flour.

## Measuring Jug

These are usually glass, but you can get plastic ones. Perfect for measuring all your liquids, such as milk, water, and even oil for cakes. They have the measures on the side, usually in millimeters (ml) and liters (l), but they can also have pints and fluid ounces (fl oz).

# KITCHEN CONVERSIONS

**1 GALLON**
4 QUARTS
8 PINTS
16 CUPS
128 OUNCES
3.8 LITERS

**1 QUART**
2 PINTS
4 CUPS
32 OUNCES
950 ML

**1 PINT**
2 CUPS
16 OUNCES
480 ML

**1 CUP**
16 TBSP
8 OUNCES
240 ML

**1/2 CUP**
8 TBSP
4 OUNCES
120 ML

**1/4 CUP**
4 TBSP
2 OUNCES
60 ML

**1 OUNCE**
2 TBSP
30 ML

**1 TBLSP**
3 TSP
1/2 OUNCE
15 ML

**1 TSP**
5 ML

## Wooden Spoons

These are a staple in every kitchen! They won't scratch your non-stick pots and pans and tend to last a really long time. You can get wooden spoons in different sizes and lengths, which are really cheap!

## Spatula

There are different types of spatula. You may have seen two key ones at home: the baking spatula with a bendy rubber head used when making cakes - when you need to scrape all the yummy mix out of the bowl. The other is a fish spatula used to flip pancakes, eggs, and burgers in a pan. If you're using a non-stick frying pan, you must invest in a good-quality plastic-style spatula so that you don't damage the non-stick coating. Remember, we are avoiding the burn!

## Peeler

These handy little tools make peeling vegetables a breeze. You can also use them to shave cheese or to make beautiful vegetable ribbons for your salads. There are a couple different types. To be honest, you will end up buying and trying both. Find your favorite; this is down to personal preference and what you mainly use it for; some are more comfortable to hold than others!

## Whisk

I still use a fork to whisk up scrambled eggs. For other jobs, such as making sauces, a whisk will make the job go much faster and leave you with a sauce or dressing that is beautifully mixed. Whisks are also best used when combining baking ingredients or when making pancakes!

**Tongs**

A pair of tongs will help you to flip over things that are too big for your fish spatula. You can also use them to help move items around in your pan; a great example would be when frying sausages or bacon. I also use tongs to serve food on the table, like roast potatoes. You can also get a longer style of tongs which are perfect for outdoor grilling (barbeques).

## DISHES AND OTHER GADGETS

Some must-have tools and other helpful gadgets to add that extra pizzazz to your kitchen experience!

**Cutting Board**

A good cutting board (chopping board) protects your knives and countertops when preparing meals. You can choose wood, plastic, or glass chopping boards. You can also buy these in sets. Some of which have different sizes and colors. This is great for preventing cross-contamination if you're cooking both meat and poultry with vegetables. In hospitality, they use specific colors for specific foods; examples include; a red chopping board for raw meat and green for salads and fruits.

## Bowls

A set of preparation bowls in your kitchen will help you organize and mix your ingredients as you cook. Although you can buy them individually, I recommend buying them as a set in different sizes. You can get plastic bowls, but I prefer glass. They are eco-friendly, microwave-friendly, and can double up as serving bowls. Tip: Items that double up as something else are beneficial when you only have a small kitchen with not much cupboard space.

## Colander

A colander will help you drain pasta and vegetables. It will also help you remove the liquid from canned beans and wash your vegetables. These are available in stainless steel and plastic.

## Can Opener

Did you know that the can opener was invented almost 50 years after the can was invented (Eschner, 2017)? There's no need to struggle with opening cans! You can find a variety of can openers in stores, from manual to electric. The one you choose may depend on your budget. Tip: More expensive doesn't always mean better; some cheaper, more basic designs work better and last longer, so start with a cheaper metal one!

### Grater

I'm a big fan of a box grater. There are four sides, and each will give you a different texture. You'll be able to zest lemons and limes, grate ginger, and shred (grate) cheese. Tip: Don't buy shredded (grated) cheese; you will pay more. Shred it yourself. It only takes a minute.

### Stick or Immersion Blender

This handy little gadget will puree your vegetables in the pot, leaving you with a delicious soup. They're also handy for making healthy breakfast smoothies and blending homemade salad dressings.

### Salad Spinner

Using a colander to dry your leafy salad greens works well, but a salad spinner takes it to the next level. Your lettuce will be really dry, which will help the salad dressing stick to it much better. You will also help to prevent soggy sandwiches and wraps!

Now that we've looked at what you'll need to start your kitchen, let's explore one of the most important skills you'll need.

## KNIFE SKILLS

Preparing your ingredients will involve cutting and slicing, so you'll have to know how to use your knives properly. Having some basic knife skills will help you to prevent injuries and will help speed up the preparation stage of cooking.

**Getting to Grips With Your Knife**

Holding your knife correctly and knowing where to put your fingers is crucial for your safety. Your index finger and thumb should be at the back of the blade, while the remaining fingers should wrap around the handle. This way, you will have a firm grip and the greatest amount of control.

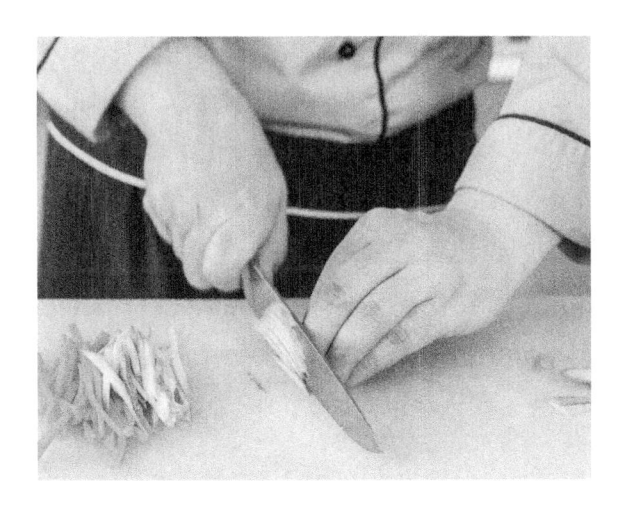

When you start chopping, you need to be steady with whatever you're chopping. Don't lay your fingers flat on the onion, cabbage, or whatever ingredient you're working with. Doing so puts you at a greater risk of cutting yourself.

Form a claw with your hand, keeping your fingertips away from the blade. Using this method, you'll protect your fingers and have more control over your actions.

**Cutting Properly**

Most people use a slicing motion or chop down on the cutting board quite fiercely when cutting their vegetables. Not only does this damage your chopping board, but also your knife!

You need to use a rocking motion with your knife to get the most even cut. If your knife is sharpened correctly, you won't even need to use much pressure at all.

**Dicing**

Diced onions are a common ingredient in recipes. You might also need to dice other vegetables, but we'll use an onion to explain the proper dicing method.

To start, cut the onion in half from the root end using your chef's knife. Make sure that you peel off the outer papery layers of the onion.

Lay the onion half flat on your chopping board and support it—remember to keep your fingertips away from the blade by making a claw with your hand.

Make a few horizontal slices into the onion, but not the whole way through (your knife needs to be sharp). Then make a few vertical slices.

Making sure that any loose pieces stay together, begin chopping the onion to get perfect dice shapes.

You might make a bit of a mess the first few times, but you'll start getting better with practice!

**Mincing**

The most common thing you'll be mincing is garlic. Sure, you can buy already minced garlic at the supermarket, but there's nothing quite like fresh garlic!

Remove one clove and chop off the hard end at the root if you've bought a whole garlic bulb. Put the clove on your chopping board and lie your chef's knife flat on top of the clove. Using your fist, smash down on your knife. This will help you to peel away the thin, papery skin. Alternatively, you could shake the garlic in a closed container, and the peels should come straight off.

Chop your garlic as finely as possible. The finer the mince, the more flavor will be released when it's being cooked.

You can buy a garlic press that will do this for you, but there is always a bit of garlic left in the press that still needs dicing. The press is also awkward to get clean afterward.

**Chiffonade**

You'll likely use this cutting technique for garnishes and salads, such as herbs and other leafy greens.

Stack your washed greens in a pile and roll them into a tight cigar shape. Thinly slice across the cigar shape with your knife. Depending on your comfort level and the number of leafy greens you're slicing, you can use your chef's knife or the smaller paring knife.

You'll be left with delicate ribbons of leafy greens, ready to sprinkle on your dish or toss into your salad.

**Julienne**

You'll find julienned carrots in salads, vegetable boards, and a few other recipes.

Cut your carrot into pieces that are two inches or five centimeters long. Slice a vertical piece of the carrot off to create a flat surface, and put the flat part on your chopping board.

Cut the piece of carrot into an eighth inch or a third of a centimeter slice. Pile the slices on top of each other and do the same.

You'll end up with sliced carrots that look like perfect matchsticks!

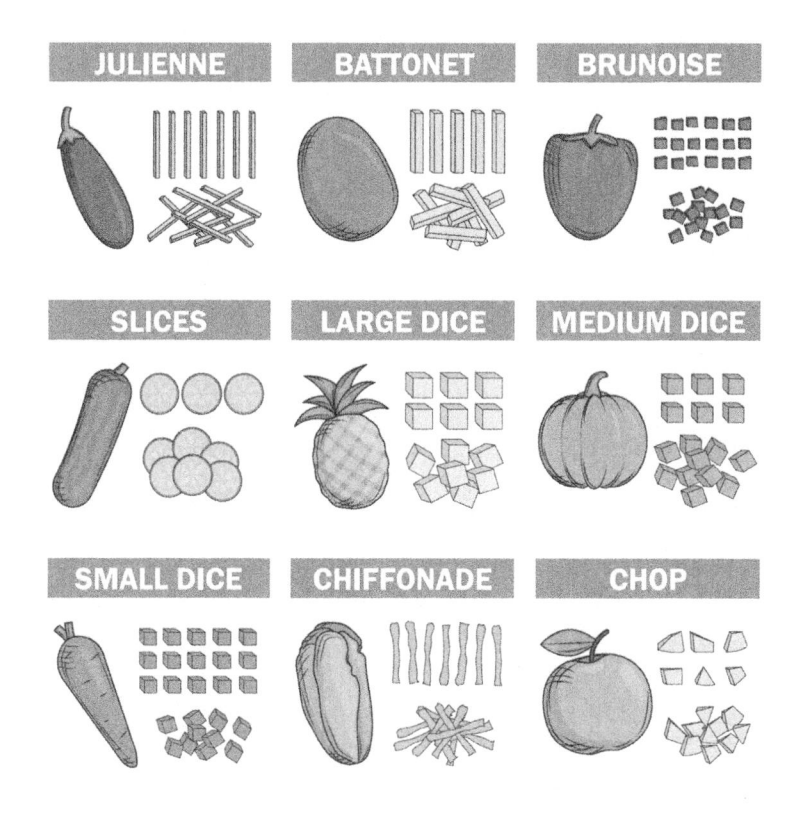

| JULIENNE | BATTONET | BRUNOISE |
| --- | --- | --- |
| SLICES | LARGE DICE | MEDIUM DICE |
| SMALL DICE | CHIFFONADE | CHOP |

STANDARD MEASURES IN COOKING

Some recipes measure using cups. Others use metric measurements. Sometimes it can get a little confusing!

Using your measuring cups, spoons, and jug you've bought to get started in the kitchen, let's look at how we can convert these amounts into something that makes more sense!

Your typical measuring cup set will include the following measurements:

- 1 cup
- ½ cup
- ⅓ cup
- ¼ cup
- ⅛ cup

Your measuring spoon set will have the following measurements:

- 1 tablespoon
- ½ tablespoon
- 1 teaspoon
- ½ teaspoon
- ¼ teaspoon

It can be easy to lose a cup or spoon. That's just life! The handy table below will help you to still get the correct measurements, even if a piece of your set is missing.

| 1 cup | 16 tablespoons |
|---|---|
| ½ cup | 8 tablespoons |
| ¼ cup | 4 tablespoons |
| ⅛ cup | 2 tablespoons |
| 1 tablespoon | 3 teaspoons |
| ½ tablespoon | 1 ½ teaspoon |
| 1 pinch | ⅛ teaspoon |

Your measuring jug has incremental markings for pints (fluid ounces) and liters, so it's an excellent tool for any recipe requiring more significant amounts of liquid.

COOKING TEMPERATURES

When browsing through recipes in a book or online, you'll find that they will tell you at what temperature to cook your food. Depending on where your recipe is from, you'll see temperatures in Celsius, Fahrenheit, and gas mark.

Don't be tempted to discard the recipe because you don't know what temperature you'll need to cook your food. The conversion table below will help you out.

| Fahrenheit | Celsius | Gas Mark |
|---|---|---|
| 250 F | 130 C | 1/2 |
| 275 F | 140 C | 1 |
| 300 F | 150 C | 2 |
| 325 F | 165 C | 3 |
| 350 F | 177 C | 4 |
| 375 F | 190 C | 5 |
| 400 F | 200 C | 6 |
| 425 F | 220 C | 7 |
| 450 F | 230 C | 8 |
| 457 F | 245 C | 9 |
| 500 F | 260 C | 10 |

## BASIC COOKING TERMS

Another confusing thing about recipes is all the technical terms that they use! It took me a while to figure out what they all meant. To save you time, let me share my little cooking terms cheat sheet with you.

### Al Dente

You'll see this in pasta dishes, where they'll tell you to cook it al dente. Al dente pasta is fully cooked but is still on the hard side. It's not mushy or soggy. Al dente is seen as perfectly cooked pasta. Carrots and other vegetables are often cooked al dente, too - it gives them that nice bite!

**Bake**

Cookies, cakes, and pies are baked. This is when it is cooked in the oven using dry heat.

**Beat**

To beat cream, for example, means that you mix it up very quickly to add air to it. You could use your whisk to do this.

**Boil**

Liquids are boiled. This is when you heat up liquid until you see bubbles coming up. When you boil potatoes, vegetables, or pasta, you cook them in boiling water.

**Clarify**

When you clarify a liquid, you remove any impurities, leaving a clear liquid. For example, removing unwanted particles from stock usually involves gently heating the stock and skimming the surface with a spoon to remove the unwanted floating particles. You can also strain the stock through a cloth or a fine strainer.

**Cream**

Creaming happens when you mix butter with sugar until it is light and fluffy and the sugar has dissolved. This is done by beating it at room temperature.

**Filet**

This unique cutting technique removes the bones from a piece of meat or fish.

**Fold**

It means folding a light mixture into a thicker and heavier mixture. You will see this in cake recipes.

**Fry**

Frying is cooking something with hot oil or butter; think of fried eggs or french fries! There are different methods. Deep frying, used for french fries. Shallow frying for eggs and bacon. Dry frying is used on meats that have their own fat content but are placed on a dry non-stick pan.

And air frying, where you need an air frying appliance! Tip: If just starting out, I wouldn't dry fry. Add a little spray oil. It also helps brown the meat and makes the pan easier to clean.

## Grill

In Europe, the grill is the top part of the oven; there is an element that produces high heat. In the US, this is called a broiler. The heat here comes from above. Another method is using charcoal. You can grill over an open flame, so the heat comes from below. In both instances, they use dry high heat for cooking.

## Lukewarm

This is when something is neither hot nor cold. Think of lukewarm as room temperature or slightly warmer than body temperature. You might see this term used when making bread or pizza dough. Lukewarm milk or water helps activate the yeast.

## Marinade

When you marinate meat or vegetables, you let them sit in a flavor-packed liquid for a period of time. This allows all those delicious flavors to soak in; try it with chicken!

## Pickle

Pickling is a common way to preserve meat, fruit, or vegetables by soaking them in vinegar, brine, or sugar. Depending on what you want to pickle, there is a method to suit.

## Sauté

You cook meat or vegetables quickly in a small amount of hot oil or butterfat at a high temperature until they just turn brown.

## Steam

This is where you cook your food in a pressure cooker or steamer. The tight lid traps the heat and allows the food to be cooked through just by using steam. Tip: I have a layered metal steamer (multi-pot). It uses one hob and replaces three pans. It's excellent for simultaneously cooking a range of vegetables and keeping them separate. A great addition to your kitchen!

If you watch cooking shows on TV, you'll hear all of these terms and some new ones. Feel free to add to the list!

## VITAMINS AND MINERALS

We all know that vitamins and minerals keep our bodies healthy. But what are they? And where do they come from?

We get vitamins and minerals from the food we eat every day. That's why ensuring you are eating the right foods is essential! You can also supplement them by taking vitamins in tablet or capsule form.

THE KITCHEN IS THE HEART OF THE HOME | 25

**HAIR**
Vitamins A,B complex, E,C,Folic Acid,Iron&Zinc

**SHARP HEARING**
Vitamins A,C,E,B12 Folic Acid&Biotin

**STABLE BLOOD PRESSURE**
Vitamins C,D Calcium, Potassium&Magnesium

**HEALTHY LUNGS**
Vitamins D,C,E & A

**HEALTHY LIVER**
Vitamins B12 & A

**BETTER BLADDER KIDNEY FUNCTION**
Vitamin B6,Magnesium, Potassium & Sodium

**STRONG IMMUNE SYSTEM**
Vitamins A,C,E & Zinc

**IMPROVED FERTILITY**
Omega 3 fatty acid,Zinc, Iron & Calcium

**STRONG BONES**
Vitamin D,Calcium, Magnesium,Phosphorus

**INCREASED ENERGY**
Vitamin B complex & Iron

**IMPROVE BRAIN POWER**
Omega 3 fatty acids,Vitamins E, B6,B12,D & Folic Acid

**CLEAR EYESIGHT**
Vitamins C,A ,E & B12

**HEALTHY HEART**
Omega 3 fatty acids, Vitamins B6,E,C & D

**CHOLESTEROL LEVELS**
Omaga 3 fatty acids,Fibre, Carotenoids,Vitamins C&E

**HEALTHY DIGESTION**
Fibre,Vitamins B12,C & Niacin

**NAILS**
Vitamins A,B complex, E,C,Folic Acid,Iron&Zinc

**LEVEL BLOOD SUGAR**
Vitamins B complex, C&D

**SUPPLE JOINTS**
Calcium,Vitamins C,D Omega 3 fatty acids

**HEALTHY MUSCLE TISSUE**
Vitamins B12,E,A & Iron

**CLEAR SKIN**
Vitamins A,C,E,D & Biotin

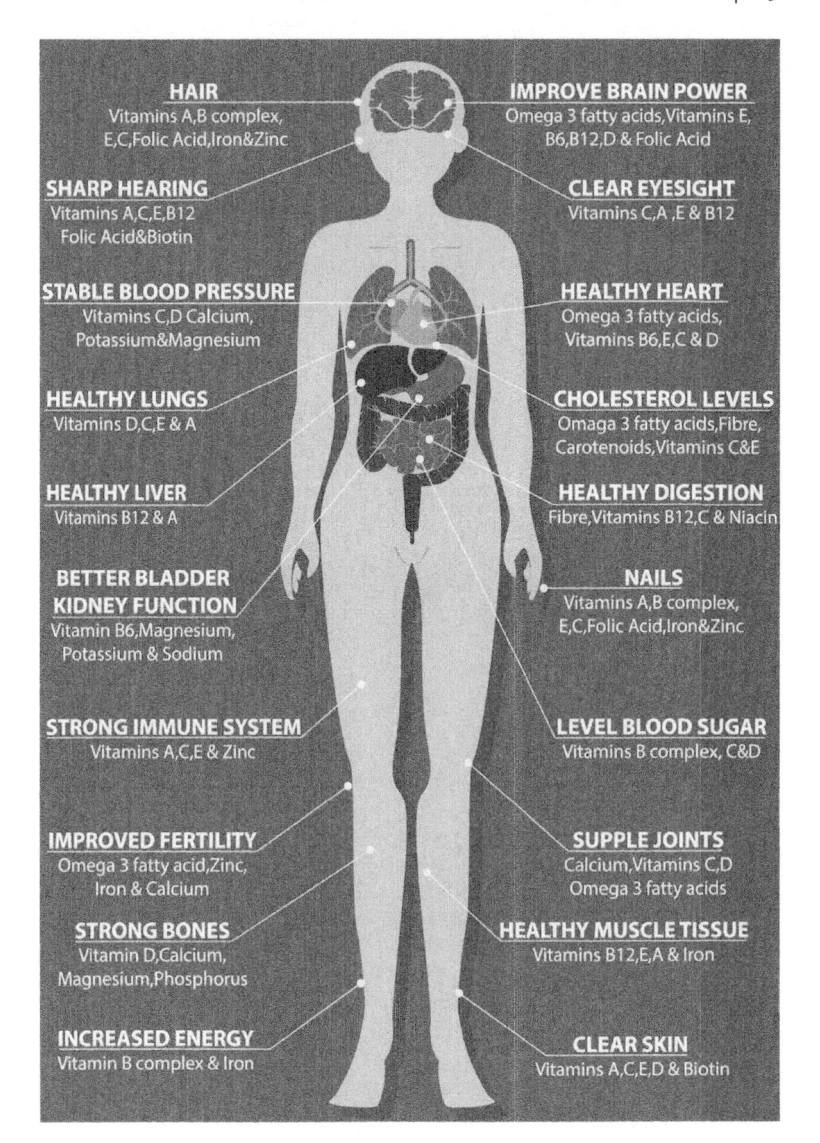

## What Are Vitamins and Minerals?

Vitamins are organic substances made by plants and animals, and there are two types.

Fat-soluble vitamins dissolve in fat and can be stored in your body. Vitamins A, D, E, and K are fat-soluble vitamins. Tip: The best source of vitamin D is from the sun! Your skin needs to be visible to soak it up! Vitamin supplements cannot give you anywhere near the amount your body needs. So getting out into the daylight is essential to boost your mood as you start getting hits from those beneficial rays.

Water-soluble vitamins dissolve in water, but your body can't store them. Therefore any vitamins that aren't absorbed into your body through your bloodstream will pass through your system. You will usually pee them out. You must ensure that you eat foods rich in these vitamins daily. Vitamins C and B-complex vitamins are water-soluble.

On the other hand, minerals are inorganic substances found in soil and water. Plants absorb the minerals, or they are eaten by animals. You'll need large amounts of some minerals while only needing a few others.

Calcium is one of the minerals you need a lot of to keep your bones healthy and strong. Copper, iron, zinc, and iodine are called trace elements because you only need a little of them at a time.

### PROTEIN, CARBS, AND FATS

There are three primary sources of nutrients, also known as "macronutrients," called carbohydrates, fats, and proteins. Your body will process carbohydrates first, then fats, then finally proteins. Understanding this process can help you manage your weight and make healthier choices for your body.

## Carbohydrates

Carbohydrates can be simple or complex. Processed foods are simple carbs that our bodies can absorb quickly, giving us quick energy boosts. Complex carbohydrates, such as those in vegetables, take longer to process.

Carbohydrates are essential for brain function. You can feel tired if the brain doesn't get enough of these carbs. Sources include; pasta, rice, potatoes, and other vegetables.

## Fat

After the carbs are absorbed, the body uses the fats. Our bodies store fats and can be used as an energy source whenever needed. Our bodies need fats such as healthy fats and oils to maintain good health. Sources include; oils, meats, and nuts.

## Protein

The last to be used is protein. Because it takes a while to get to it, proteins can make you feel less hungry for longer, so it is a good food source to have in greater quantity. Proteins are essential for bones, muscles, skin, hair, and nails. Protein also helps digestion. Sources include; meat, eggs, nuts, and beans.

## MEAL TIME IDEAS

Deciding what to eat can sometimes be as tricky as making something to eat! I have a few quick and easy recipes to try as you're starting out in your kitchen.

**Breakfast of Champions**

They say breakfast is the day's most important meal, and they're not wrong! Even if you're running late, you must get some food in your body to give you the energy to get your day started. I always think about it like fuel for a car. You wouldn't put the wrong fuel into your prized vehicle, so why do it to yourself. We deserve the best right! Skipping breakfast can lead to headaches, dizziness, and low blood sugar and can even prevent you from concentrating properly.

Here are a few quick breakfast recipes to get your day off to a good start.

**Scrambled Eggs**

You can make perfect scrambled eggs in about 10 minutes. Add a slice of toast, wholemeal is best, and you're good to go!

**Time:** 10 minutes
**Serving Size:** Makes one serving.
**Prep Time:** 5 minutes

**Cook Time:** 5 minutes

**Ingredients:**

- 4 large eggs
- ¼ cup of whole milk
- salt and pepper to taste
- 1 tablespoon of butter
- chives, parsley, or thyme (optional)

**Directions:**

1. Crack your eggs into a mixing bowl.
2. Beat them with a whisk until they become pale yellow in color.
3. Add the milk and season with salt and pepper.
4. Make sure you whisk eggs thoroughly. You want to add as much air into the mixture as possible.
5. Melt the butter in a non-stick pan on medium-low heat.
6. When the butter is hot enough, pour the egg mixture into the pan.
7. Leave the mixture to cook in the pan for about a minute.

8. Gently start mixing eggs with a spatula. Make sure that all the liquid parts start cooking. You don't need to break up the eggs too much.
9. Turn off the heat, but keep mixing until no liquid is left.
10. Dish up on a plate and enjoy!

You can add some grated cheese or diced ham to your eggs for an extra treat at step 8. You can add some additional flavor by adding fresh herbs like chives, parsley, or thyme.

**Omelet**

If you can make scrambled eggs, you can make an omelet. An omelet is a great way to start the day and makes a delicious dinner in just 10 minutes!

**Time:** 15 minutes
**Serving Size:** Makes one serving.
**Prep Time:** 5 minutes
**Cook Time:** 10 minutes

**Ingredients:**

- 2 eggs
- 1 tablespoon of butter
- 2 tablespoons of milk

- salt and pepper to taste
- ⅛ cup of grated cheese
- your choice of herbs and fillings

For fillings, you can use bacon or ham, any leftover meats, diced mushrooms, or diced tomatoes. Just remember not to overfill your omelet, as overloading can break it!

**Directions:**
1. Break your eggs into a glass bowl and whisk until they are pale yellow in color.
2. Add the milk and season with salt and pepper.
3. Make sure you whisk your eggs thoroughly. You want to add as much air into the mixture as possible.
4. Melt the butter in a non-stick pan on medium-low heat.
5. When the butter is hot enough, pour the egg mixture into the pan.
6. Leave the mixture to cook in the pan for about a minute.
7. With a rubber spatula, carefully push one edge of the egg mixture toward the middle of the pan while tilting it slightly. This will move the liquid mixture's parts into that spot.
8. Repeat step 7 a few times in different areas around the edge to ensure that all the liquid is cooked.

9. Your egg mixture should now look like a yellow pancake and should move around the pan easily. If it's a little stuck, gently use your spatula to loosen it.
10. Carefully flip your egg pancake to let it cook on the other side.
11. Add your cheese and other fillings by placing them in a line in the center of the egg pancake.
12. With your spatula, gently fold the egg pancake (omelet) in half to wrap your fillings up. Make sure that it doesn't start going brown.
13. Carefully move your omelet onto a plate, garnish with some extra herbs and enjoy!

**Pancakes**

Pancakes take a little longer to make, so they are a delicious weekend breakfast! We'll be garnishing the pancakes with mixed berries in this recipe, but you can be more decadent and use chocolate chips instead. In 45 minutes, you'll be enjoying delicious, fluffy pancakes!

**Time:** 30 minutes
**Serving Size:** Makes 10–12 pancakes.
**Prep Time:** 10 minutes
**Cook Time:** 20 minutes

**Ingredients:**

- 2 cups of all-purpose (plain) flour
- 2 tablespoons of baking powder
- 2 large eggs
- 2 cups of milk
- 2 tablespoons of sugar
- 1 teaspoon of fine salt
- 1 teaspoon of pure vanilla extract
- 2 tablespoons of butter (optional)
- 2 cups of mixed berries
- Maple syrup to garnish

**Directions:**

1. In a large mixing bowl, sift, or whisk the flour and baking powder together.
2. Break the eggs into a separate bowl and beat them well.
3. Add the milk, sugar, and salt to the eggs and mix well.
4. Add the vanilla extract to the egg mixture and mix.
5. Add the egg mixture to the flour and mix for about 30 seconds. You can break up some

bigger lumps, but don't worry about the smaller ones.
6. Let the mixture rest for about 15 minutes.
7. Heat a non-stick pan over medium heat.
8. Once the pan is hot, spray it with cooking spray.
9. For each pancake, pour about ¼ cup of the mixture into the pan.
10. Allow them to cook for about 2 minutes. The tops of the pancakes should have bubbles, the edges shouldn't be runny, and the bottoms should be light golden brown.
11. Flip the pancakes and allow them to cook for about a minute, then remove them from the pan.
12. Repeat steps 9–11 until the pancake mixture is finished.
13. To keep your cooked pancakes warm, put them in an oven-safe dish and keep them in a warm—but not too hot—oven.
14. Garnish your pancakes with mixed berries, maple syrup, and butter. If you don't want butter, you could try adding a dollop of creme fraiche for a bit of luxury.

## Smoothie

A smoothie is a favorite summer breakfast in my house! It takes only a few minutes to make; refreshing, delicious, and healthy!

**Time:** 5 minutes
**Serving Size:** Makes one serving.
**Prep Time:** 3 minutes
**Cook Time:** 2 minutes

**Ingredients:**

- 1 banana.
- 1 tablespoon of oats
- 80 grams or 2 and ½ ounces of soft fruit (you can use strawberries, blueberries, or mango).
- ½ cup of milk (can be cow's milk, almond, oat, or whatever you prefer)
- 1 teaspoon of honey
- 1 teaspoon of vanilla extract

**Directions:**

1. Put all the ingredients in a bowl or jug.

2. Use your stick blender to blend for one minute or until the mixture is smooth.
3. Serve and enjoy!

Smoothies are great to enjoy en route to college or work, especially if you walk in.

Tip 1: When your bananas get too ripe, peel them, wrap them in a freezer bag, and then freeze them. Come next, smoothie time; you can chuck them in. They will be lovely and sweet and chill the smoothie!

Tip 2: Keep a bag of frozen berries in your freezer, ready to go.

LUNCH OR DINNER

What do you eat while you're at school or work? Getting a daily meal from the shop around the corner is quick and easy, but buying ready-made meals can be a little expensive! The meals I'm sharing here are easy to make and travel well. You can enjoy them at your desk, on the lawn, or in the comfort of your own home.

**Salads**

Making food doesn't always have to involve using the oven or stovetop. You can throw together a quick, refreshing salad on hot summer days and evenings in no time!

**Time:** 10 minutes
**Serving Size:** Makes one family-size serving.
**Prep Time:** 5 minutes
**Cook Time:** 5 minute

**Ingredients:**

- A leafy green base. Use two or three types of lettuce to have some variety in your salad. Chop your lettuce into bite-sized pieces.
- Tomatoes. Choose the tomatoes that are in season. You can slice them or chop them into smaller pieces. Tip: I like cherry tomatoes. I leave them whole as they stay fresher longer.
- Additional vegetables like onions, cucumber, green, red, or yellow bell peppers, carrots, or celery. I like to make my salads colorful!
- Protein like shredded chicken or bacon. Salads are a great way of using leftover meats!
- Cheese, for example, feta cheese or grated cheddar cheese.

- Nuts and seeds, like walnuts, almonds, or pumpkin seeds.

Be careful not to overload your salad too much. Think about the flavors you want, and make sure that your ingredients follow along!

**Directions:**

1. Wash your lettuce thoroughly and make sure it's as dry as possible using your colander, paper towels, or salad spinner.
2. Layer your chosen ingredients in a bowl.
3. Add the salad dressing before serving so that your lettuce doesn't wilt.
4. Serve and enjoy!

If you want to take your salad to work or school, layer your ingredients heaviest at the bottom, and the lettuce at the very top. This will help to keep your lettuce fresh and crispy. Make sure you take your salad dressing in a separate container!

**Baked Salmon**

This will do the trick if you want to look fancy for lunch or dinner with minimal effort.

**Time:** 30 minutes
**Serving Size:** Makes four servings.
**Prep Time:** 10 minutes
**Cook Time:** 20 minutes

**Ingredients:**

- 2 pounds (900 grams) of salmon
- a few sprigs of rosemary
- 2 lemons, sliced
- 2 tablespoons olive oil
- 1 teaspoon salt
- ½ teaspoon black pepper
- 4 garlic cloves, peeled and hopped

**Directions:**

1. Leave your salmon out of the fridge for a few minutes to get to room temperature.
2. On a sheet of foil, add a thin coat of olive oil, half of your rosemary, and half of your lemon. Place salmon onto the lemon and rosemary.
3. Sprinkle olive oil, salt, pepper, and garlic onto the salmon and rub it in.
4. Add the remaining rosemary and lemon on top of the salmon and enclose it in the foil.

5. Bake for 15–20 minutes at 180 degrees Celsius or 350 degrees Fahrenheit.
6. Remove the salmon from the foil and open the top part. Turn your oven to broil (grill) and add it back to the oven for three minutes until golden brown.

Voilà! Just like that, you have a fancy and nutritious meal prepared so quickly. It is important to note that cooking time may vary depending on the thickness of your salmon. Always ensure it is cooked through at the thickest part.

FOOD PRESERVATION

Preserving your food is an excellent way of saving money. It minimizes the growth of bacteria and pathogens, keeps your food from spoiling too quickly, and ensures that it is preserved at its best.

There are many ways to preserve your food. For example, if you have fresh herbs, you can wrap them in paper towels and close them in an airtight container. This will extend the lifespan of the herbs in your fridge for up to three weeks.

Chilling and freezing are the most common ways of preserving items, and putting items in your fridge or freezer will dramatically increase the product's lifespan. Some fruits and vegetables, such as apples, bananas, and onions, should not be placed near each other or other fruit and vegetables due to the gas produced. They will ripen and spoil too quickly. Try storing them separately to prolong their life.

You can also sugar fresh produce by covering it with sugar syrup. Sugar prevents the growth and buildup of bacteria.

Salting your food also allows you to preserve it. Dry it out with salt, or store it in a wet brine or pickling vinegar, which can also be used for canning items.

Lastly, you can also vacuum seal your food to keep it from going bad.

SHOPPING TIPS

When you start shopping for yourself, there are many things to consider. After all, you will have a budget that you will need to stick to. Here are some tips that you can use when you go shopping for groceries (Pepper, 2012):

- Don't go grocery shopping when you're hungry; you will buy all the wrong things and go wildly over budget!
- Check "use by" dates on all perishable items, fridge items, and bread. Make sure the items will still be "in date" when you plan to use them.
- Save the frozen goods for last, so they don't get warm while shopping.
- Compare the prices of different brands.
- Meat items may be marked down at the end of the day. Do your shopping in the evening.
- Expensive items are always placed at eye level. Be sure to check all shelves.
- If you have the space, buy non-perishable items in bulk. You can freeze meals and make meal prep an absolute breeze.
- Plan meals and the ingredients you will need in advance.
- Make a shopping list and stick to it!
- Check your mail and newspapers for coupons (vouchers).

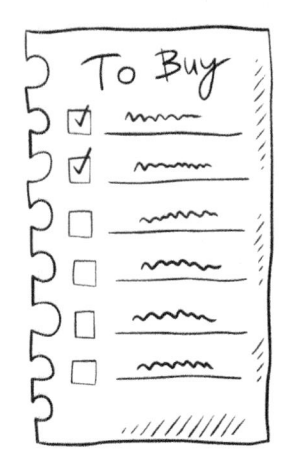

- Don't be tricked by "three for the price of two" specials if you only need one item. The rest will go to waste because you have no use for them.
- Use the calculator on your phone to see how much you are up to on your grocery budget.

**Best Before vs. Use Before Date**

The "best before" date on packaging refers to food quality.

**Food Storage: expiration dates**

**USE BY** — USE BY 24 AUG
you've got until the end of this date to use or freeze the food before it becomes too risky to eat

vs.

**BEST BEFORE** — BEST BEFORE 16 OCT
you can eat food past this date but it might not be at its best quality

Food quality diminishes over time. The "best before" date implies that the quality of that food item will not be as high after the date stated. If you have food in your fridge past its "best before" date, do not just throw it out. If unopened or stored correctly, it still may be perfectly fresh; use common sense here.

The "use before" date refers to food safety. These are usually items that need to be stored optimally and have properties that may be compromised if kept longer than the recommended date.

Medications are marked as "use before." It is advisable to heed the dates and dispose of these items when those dates have expired.

**Nutritional Facts (Information)**

While nutritional facts on food packaging may change over time as legislation changes. The critical messaging and facts remain mostly consistent. Providing details on calories per serving, serving size, and a breakdown of nutrients such as fat, carbohydrates (sugar), protein, and vitamin content. It also includes your recommended daily value (allowance) of each nutrient, vitamin, and mineral with that product's percentage of the daily allowance it delivers. There will also be an ingredients table that should highlight included common allergens in bold.

**Growing Your Own Foods**

The nice thing about some edible plants is that you can plant them right on your windowsills. Providing they get enough sunlight and water, you can grow;

- cress on your windowsill, which is great to add to salads.
- pea shoots which can be added to stir fry.
- a variety of herbs, such as basil, cilantro (coriander), and arugula (parsley), will make your kitchen smell wonderful.
- kale and edible flowers such as chives and calendula.

You can either start these off as seeds, buy young seedling plants or buy already-grown plants and take care of them, taking cuttings when needed. It's up to you! They all take a bit of nurturing.

## WATER INTAKE

Something that often gets forgotten is drinking water. Water is vital for our overall health and well-being. We need to drink water to stay healthy because water makes up approximately 75% of our bodies. If you have remained consistent with your water intake, you probably get annoyed with how often you have to run to the loo. But water is a must. Depending on your build, you will need to consume approximately 2-3 liters daily. If you struggle to drink your daily water intake, you can try infusing your water with lemon, mint, and cucumbers. You could add berries and sip on naturally flavored water throughout the day.

Alternatively, you can purchase water drops that add flavor to your water. Tip: Get yourself a large water bottle, either 1 or 2 liters. Buy one that you love the look and feel of. You can track how much you have drunk, and because you love the bottle, you are more likely to use it and show it off!

# 2

## KEEPING YOUR HOME CLEAN—
## THE TOOLS YOU NEED AND HOW
## TO USE THEM

We all know how important it is to keep a home clean and tidy. We know that our parents and families would nag us to clean up our rooms or force us to clean the house and wash the dishes, and I can almost guarantee that we never stopped to wonder why.

You see, from a scientific perspective, keeping your home clean and tidy is crucial not only for our mental well-being but also our physical well-being. Decluttering your home allows you to actively reduce your stress and anxiety.

You may find your mind overstimulated when your space is untidy and dirty. You focus on moving the clutter around rather than on the task. This leads to excessive stress. But keeping your home clean and clutter-free is enough to avoid and bypass this stress entirely.

From a physical perspective, keeping your home consistently clean and tidy will reduce the build-up of allergens in your home that stem from dust. You will also prevent an infestation of pests and vermin because cleaning your home means you leave nothing for the little critters to feast on.

Also, one of the greatest benefits of keeping your home clean is that you don't have to spring clean or do more significant cleaning tasks. Doing a little bit each day goes a long way.

For example, if you have just eaten breakfast, wash up your single dish and wipe down the counter where you have prepared your meal and where you have eaten. You can go about your day without a second thought. If you do this each time you eat or use a dish or utensil, you will prevent a complete build-up of dishes in the sink and grime on the countertops. And this will mean no bugs and critters snooping around for any leftovers.

Have you ever heard of someone being called a "scatterbrain"? When your environment is cluttered, you may find it challenging to focus. While moving around cups or papers, you are not getting any work done.

Think about how it is almost impossible to sleep on your bed if laundry is scattered over it. If you have a neat and clean environment, it creates a soothing space for you to function.

The main benefit of cleaning on the go in small bursts is saving time in the long run. You don't have to spend an entire weekend cleaning your space from top to bottom because there won't be anything to clean. This way, everything is always kept well-organized. You may be surprised at how easy it is to find the keys you always seem to be losing under the heap of chip (crisp) packets on your coffee table.

## WHAT TO GIVE, WHAT TO KEEP

It is easy to talk about decluttering your space, but where would you even begin? The reality is that it's so easy to accumulate stuff—even if you think you are successfully pulling off the minimalist vibe in your home. While everything may look tidy, I can almost guarantee that there is a closet or cabinet in absolute chaos somewhere in your home. It is also probably the space you are trying the hardest to avoid because it makes you nervous just thinking about it.

The good news is that there are ways of tackling these spaces without becoming too overwhelmed. Chances are you are heading off to college or moving out of your home into a new apartment. This already means that you are winning! You are starting with a clean slate, and all you have to do is make sure that you maintain your new space so that it doesn't become a problem every week.

**Clothing Items**

It is easy to build up clutter over time, so let us start with clothes. I have often found that clothes are a primary source of clutter. Styles and fashion change, and while it seems like it's happening slowly, two years have gone by, and at the back of your closet sits the jeans that you would neither wear out in public nor that would fit you. And there is no shame in that.

However, the build-up of clothes in cupboards is not great for our mental health. Squeezing into those old pairs of jeans takes just as much emotional stress as physical strain. But a way to solve this problem is to start with all clothing items hung on hangers. January 1st rolls around, and instead of making any new year's resolutions you won't stick to, turn your clothing hangers with the hook facing the same direction. As you wear clothing items and hang them back in the closet, turn the hangers to face the other direction.

Look at the hangers near the end of the season or the end of the year. Ones that have not been turned around have not been worn. Let's be honest; if you didn't wear those items for a whole year, what are the chances of you ever wearing them again?

The same can be done with folded clothing items instead of hung items. The way to do this is to change how they are folded or rolled in your cupboard or drawer, and if you have room, move them to one side. If you decide to use this method, pack your clothing items so that it is easy to see everything. The last thing you want is to find some t-shirts or jeans at the back of your closet telling you it's time to part ways because you haven't worn those items in a year, just because you forgot you had them (the "out of sight, out of mind" trap)!

Now that you have seen what you do and don't use, you can peacefully part ways with the items you haven't worn in 365 days. What do you do with these clothing items? I advise finding your nearest charity drive, store, or clothing bank and donating the clothes to those less fortunate.

## Clothing Organization

**Sell** — Nice clothes in perfect condition that you don't wear for a long time

**Trash** — Things in bad condition from non-recyclable materials

**Recycle** — Recyclable clothes in poor condition

**Keep and Organize** — Your favorite clothes in good condition

**Donate** — Clothes in good contition that you don't like or don't wear for a long time

If you're anything like me, you may look lovingly at a pair of jeans you haven't worn in a year, and the thought of keeping them crosses your mind. Don't fall into the trap. If you want a similar pair in years to come, or if this style makes a comeback, I guarantee you can walk into a store and pick up a pair. If not, you just saved yourself some closet space.

## Non-Clothing Items

The same rule of thumb that I use for clothing items is the same rule of thumb that I use for non-clothing items. Do you know the "drawer" that seems to exist in every family home? I'm talking about the one with the pair of scissors, the random ball of yarn, paperclips, broken fridge magnets, and about 100 other things that have not been used in years. Yes, that drawer! When you move out on your own, it will be easy to find yourself two months down the line with the same drawer forming.

Again, I like to apply the one-year rule to these items. If I haven't used it in a year, it needs to be tossed, and if I find myself needing it in a few months, I can head to the store and buy a new one, although this rarely happens.

### CLEANING THE HOUSE

Now, something equally as important as decluttering and keeping your home tidy—although slightly different—is keeping your home clean. I know this may seem confusing, especially when you thought clean and tidy was the same thing. But they are actually two different components.

Tidying your home means decluttering. Everything in your home has an assigned space, and when you use each item, you pack it back into its designated space. No random items are lying around your home, making things look more full or cluttered than they are. Clutter can create the illusion of making everything in our homes seem "dirty."

On the other hand, cleaning means actively removing dirt and germs from your home. Let me give you an example. Think about your bathroom for a second. Tidying means putting away your toothbrush and toothpaste, hair products lying around the wash basin, shampoo and conditioner, and anything else back into your bathroom cabinet. Cleaning would mean using a disinfectant soap to wipe down all the surfaces, removing toothpaste, grime build-up, and hair! It means using a toilet cleaner and disinfectant to clean the inside of your toilet and the toilet seat. I know this isn't enjoyable to hear, but it needs to be done. I advise doing this before taking a lovely, luxurious, and long shower.

Let us look a bit closer at cleaning and its benefits.

## THE BENEFITS OF CLEANING

Many people choose to have a day in the week dedicated to cleaning their homes. This is the day when they are up bright and early; they grab their supplies and get straight to it. Perhaps you know what I'm talking about—weekend mornings with your mom calling you to come and help clean or vacuum the home, which usually means interrupted sleep. Whichever you're familiar with, it was undoubtedly not how you thought you'd spend your weekend morning. But it goes without saying that cleaning is essential as much as it annoys you. Aside from the obvious benefits that cleaning poses, such as having a healthy environment and an aesthetically pleasing home, you being the one to clean your home poses multiple benefits.

**Good Exercise**

Cleaning your home allows you to put some elbow grease into cleaning it. If you're studying for college exams or working a part-time job, you are not even thinking about heading to the gym. Cleaning your home involves a lot of "heavy lifting." You will be moving a sofa and maybe your bed too. This allows you to get some strength exercises in. You will be bending, swishing your arms from side to side, and doing a lot of walking. You may not be getting the fully-fledged workout you'd get at the gym, but you may get in a great cardio workout. In fact, some studies have found that you could burn up to 100 calories while vacuuming or cleaning your windows. The mere fact that you are moving is already a "step" in the right direction.

**Helps You Concentrate**

You know the feeling of procrastination, right? You'd rather be doing anything except the task at hand. When faced with that particular feeling, it is tempting to start picking up bits of paper, grabbing a wipe, and removing all the specs of dust in sight. Just so you can avoid doing what you actually have to do. When you clean your home often, you remove the distractions that keep you from doing work, even when you consider them as welcomed distractions.

When everything is clean and tidy and in its proper place, it is easier to concentrate and focus on getting work done.

**You Can Eat Healthier**

There is a direct relationship between stress and what we put in our bodies. When you're preparing for an examination, you are more likely to want to snack on junk food than you are to snack on fruits or vegetables. The reason for this is that our bodies respond to stress by seeking out comfort foods. So naturally, if your environment is causing stress by being full of junk and dirt, it will impact your eating habits. If you keep your home clean and tidy, you may help yourself without even realizing it, and you'll eat healthier.

**You Will Sleep Better**

If you're anything like me, you need a constant reminder of what you need to do. For example, if I need to top up on milk, I will leave the empty carton on the table to remind myself that I need to get more milk. When working on a project, I usually have multiple tabs open on my browser so I don't forget what I am researching. Now, if you find yourself doing this in your virtual space, you may also find yourself doing this in your physical space. This means that all around your home and your room are small reminders of what you need to do. Imagine getting ready to turn in for the night, with little reminders all around your room of things you are yet to do. That could be very distracting, right? If you've cleaned and tidied up your bedroom, the chances of your mind being calm are much higher than being surrounded by dirt and clutter.

**"Cleaner Home" equals "Better Health"**

The cleaner your home is, the better you will feel overall. Not because everything looks pristine and generally healthier but because the less clutter you have, the easier it is to keep surfaces clean and disinfected. It is also essential to vacuum your carpets, clean your floors, and all other general surfaces in your home. This is because dirt and germs get trapped in the not-so-easy-to-clean places and surfaces, posing an unhealthy breathing environment. Think about it this way, how much dust would get trapped in a carpet as opposed to a tiled or wooden floor? It is much easier to wipe off the tile or wooden floor germs than to clean a carpet. Therefore, doing a deep cleaning by vacuuming is extremely important.

## HOW TO CLEAN YOUR SPACE

So now that I have explained the benefits of cleaning your space, many of which I'm sure you're already familiar with, you probably have many questions about how to actually clean it. Where would you even begin, and most importantly, how could you possibly keep track of all these chores all the time?

Your starting point is to pick a designated time that you are going to clean. Don't choose a time before you head out with your friends for dinner because I can assure you that you would choose time with your friends over cleaning, which may lead to you doing a less thorough job. Once you have selected a time, you need to know if you are doing a complete and thorough cleaning or if you are maintaining what you have already cleaned. My advice is to designate time for both.

What I mean by a complete and thorough cleaning is sweeping, dusting, vacuuming, washing, and wiping all in one go. On the other hand, maintenance would mean just sweeping or wiping off surfaces you have used most often or decluttering spaces that have gathered clutter.

The next thing you will do is complete an entire task in all the rooms of your home instead of completing a single room entirely. For example, when sweeping, you will do so throughout your home. When you vacuum, you will do so throughout your home. And when you mop, you will do so throughout your entire space. You're not going to sweep, vacuum, and mop one room at a time. This makes it more taxing on you physically, and you may find yourself getting tired halfway through and ending up with half a clean house and half a dirty place, and nobody wants that.

Nothing is more annoying or frustrating than getting into the vibe of cleaning, your playlist is ready, and you are more motivated than ever. Still, you can't find your cleaning supplies. Or you have your mop, but you can't find your broom. That is enough to bring your motivation down to zero. The best way to solve this problem is to keep all your cleaning supplies together. Whether it is a caddy, a cupboard, or even a bag, having all your cleaning supplies and equipment together makes it easy to maintain motivation when the moment strikes.

**The Cleaning Order**

Suppose it's the first time you're cleaning a space by yourself, whether in your apartment, house, or dorm room. Figuring out where to start may be challenging, especially without being told what to do and where to find whatever you are looking for. This, coupled with the fact that you are in more of a time crunch when you are living on your own than when you are helping your mom, means that the stakes are high. You want to clean the place as soon as possible and correctly.

Before wiping or disinfecting, you will go through your home tidying up the clutter. You are going to pack things away, throw things out, or place them in a designated area in your home where you keep all items that you are hoping to donate (Nationwide, 2020).

If you have them ensure that all fans are off in your home, so it doesn't spread any dust you have just wiped away. You are then going to start with wiping off countertops and the objects on the countertops, which may include things like appliances, decorative artifacts, mirrors, and other small items. You will then move on to sweeping the floor and then mopping or washing the floor.

When it comes to carpets, these can be vacuumed once or twice a week, and you can consider a deep cleaning either once or twice a year.

When you get to the kitchen and the bathroom area of your home, it is always good to heed the "let it soak" advice. First, use a toilet cleaner and a kitchen cleaner and let it soak in the wash basins and toilets for a little while. Then using some elbow grease and a brush to thoroughly clean these surfaces.

I know cleaning seems like a drag, and it may feel like the worst part of adulthood. Still, once it becomes a part of your routine, it happens without you thinking much about it and interfering with your social plans.

## THE TOILET

The toilet is an essential part of the home that makes people cringe when they think about cleaning. Yes, you can quickly disinfect and clean the surfaces within your bathroom, but the toilet seems like it's in a league of its own. It's almost as though we expect it to need some sort of special treatment when in actual fact, it's just as easy to clean as any other part of our home.

Before treating the throne in your home, ensure that you have a toilet brush permanently located next to the toilet and a product to clean it with. This can be toilet cleaners that you have purchased from the store, or it could even be vinegar.

Next, when you pour your toilet cleaner into the toilet pan, you're going to make sure to give it a little bit of a swish around first to ensure every part of the toilet gets a touch of the cleaner. Then, you're going to leave it to sit in the toilet for a little while. I like to start the bathroom cleaning process by doing this, then cleaning the rest of the bathroom and returning to the toilet afterward. This gives the toilet cleaner enough time to sit and work on the stubborn stains or grime that may have formed.

It's always great to have a toilet cleaner, disinfectant spray, or sanitizing spray that can be used around the outer area of the toilet and on the toilet seat. Remember, we are not just focusing on cleaning the inside of the toilet.

Next, you must clean the area around the toilet's base. This may be the bathroom floor area you hope to mop up at some point, but this shouldn't be neglected.

And lastly, the part of the toilet that I can guarantee most people forget to clean, myself included, is the cistern part of the toilet. Not only is it unseen, but there are so many mechanics there that you're probably worried something may dislodge or break. But do not neglect this area. It is constantly filled with water and can be a breeding ground for bacteria. Be sure to remove the lid and clean the underside of the lid, as well as any mold build-up that may have accumulated (Molly Maid, n.d.).

**Fixing a Leaking Toilet**

Whether you fancy yourself a DIY enthusiast or not, there are some basic house maintenance pointers that you should know. I have friends who lost their parents at a young age. Aside from missing their parents dearly, their most significant challenge was that they depended on their parents to do things for them. With them gone, they felt stranded and alone, suddenly expected to know everything their parents knew.

When you're out on your own, you will face difficulties alone. One such difficulty is a leaky toilet. The constant sound is annoying, and the water leak, if your water is metered, can cause your water bill to skyrocket. You don't need the added expense. Tip: It's also highly beneficial to have emergency numbers on your phone or fridge where they are easy to see. These are not just emergency numbers for the ambulance or police but also a 24-hour plumber in your area, electrician, and other handypersons that you may need to call for immediate help.

As time progresses, the flapper inside the toilet tank wears out. The flapper is the seal that releases water into the bowl when you flush. Water won't stop flowing into the bowl if this essential yet small component is compromised. Albeit in small and slow trickles, the cistern will be constantly refilled. To change the flapper, turn off the water supply and flush the toilet to empty the tank. You can then remove the old flapper. If unsure of the size, it is always a good idea to take the old, worn one to the store to purchase the correct replacement. Installation should be as easy as removal.

## THE SHOWER HEAD

There is nothing that can ruin your morning quite like a shower head that is trickling out droplets of water ever so slowly. It feels like it takes forever to rinse the shampoo out of your hair, and you're mostly cold because the warm water isn't covering nearly enough of your body. If you move into any new place, it is almost always guaranteed that the previous owners or tenants didn't clean the showerhead. This leaves you with the task of doing it yourself.

There are two options here: first is filling a zip lock bag with vinegar and tying it to your shower head, allowing your shower head to get cleaned without actually removing it, and the second option is removing the entire shower head with a wrench, or it may unscrew by hand and letting it soak in white vinegar or apple cider vinegar, and scrubbing off the mineral and soap build-up. While the second option is more effective than the first, both yield noticeable results.

If the toilet or showerhead problem seems too complicated and isn't resolved through cleaning, don't be ashamed to call in a plumber, your building's superintendent, or your landlord.

CLEANING THE OVEN

We've all faced the slow build-up of grime in our oven that seems to accumulate so gradually it almost appears out of nowhere. And as you're cleaning your home, the irksome dirt seems to taunt you. You may avoid this because you don't know where to start cleaning your oven. Don't worry. I have you covered.

Before you start deep cleaning, you first need to make sure that you remove any and all removable parts from the oven. The oven racks and any oven dishes that may be stored in your oven will come out, as these parts can easily be cleaned in the sink.

To begin with, the best way to avoid any grime build-up is to wipe up any spills and overflows as and when they happen. Now, don't decide to wipe the oven while it's still piping hot. Instead, use a damp cloth with some oven cleaner or dish soap to clean the oven while it is warm, not hot.

You will need a good quality oven cleaner for the more stubborn grime that has built up over time. Spray inside and outside the oven (the handles, nobs, and glass panels), and leave for about two hours. This will allow the grime to loosen up and be wiped quickly away.

An alternative, cheaper option is to use a non-chemical cleaner to clean your oven by making a paste of bicarbonate of soda and water. Spread this mixture over all the surfaces of your oven. Leave it to sit for 12 hours before wiping it away. Once wiped, spray vinegar from a spray bottle into your oven to remove residual bicarb. Wherever it fizzes up, that's where there's still some residue.

I'm sure you've heard of a self-cleaning oven, you may even have one, but I don't recommend you use this. I know, I know, but just hear me out. I am not trying to deliberately make your life hard.

Self-cleaning ovens, while they do work, they clean themselves by steaming or incinerating the grime in the oven. But this comes at a high cost. First, the potential for the oven to catch on fire is exponentially increased. You basically have to watch your oven like a hawk. Also, because it incinerates the grime build-up, it fills your home with potent odors that can be hard to eliminate.

If you are not feeling up to putting in the elbow grease, some companies offer full oven cleaning services, and they keep your oven looking good as new. All you would need to do is maintain the upkeep of the oven and keep it clean.

## CLEANING THE REFRIGERATOR

Once a month, you will need to clean your refrigerator. The sauce bottles that are long forgotten and the food that made its way to the back of the fridge, never to be seen or used again, need throwing out.

Cleaning your fridge is best done the day before your next grocery shop. This is because your fridge will be empty enough for you to unpack and unplug it. Unplugging your refrigerator will allow the freezer to defrost. Don't be tempted to use a knife to break off any ice. You may damage the freezer. Remove shelves and racks to wash in the sink. You can then wipe the inside of your fridge and freezer with a warm damp cloth. You can use a bit of soap, baking soda made into a paste mixed with water, or cider vinegar mixed with water and applied from a spray bottle.

Keeping your fridge and freezer clean and removing a build-up of ice will also extend the lifespan of your entire unit because the ice won't block any ventilation.

## LAUNDRY

For so many people, laundry is the bane of their existence. The seemingly endless flow of dirty clothes that must be washed, folded, and ironed is enough to make even the sanest people feel like they're going crazy.

If you've ever wondered how often you should be doing laundry, there is a way of figuring it out. Generally, clothes worn closer to your skin or that make direct contact with your skin will need to be washed more often. Things worn over layers or further from your skin don't need to be washed often. For example, clothing items such as socks, underwear, and undergarments should be cleaned after wearing them once. But jerseys and jackets don't need to be washed as often.

Also, the hotter the weather is, the more often you will need to wash your clothes. This is because you sweat more when it's hot. Clothes that have spills or stains on them need to be cleaned immediately. This will prevent permanent stains from being left behind.

The clothing type will also determine how often you do laundry. Jeans are washed less often, but cotton gym clothes will be cleaned more frequently.

When we talk about laundry, this also includes sheets, linens, and towels. Towels can generally be used three times before heading into the laundry basket, and sheets must be changed and washed at least once a week.

**Laundry Products to Use**

It may be overwhelming to walk into the laundry aisle at any store and see the many brands and types of detergents on the market. Especially when doing this on your own for the first time. But remember that the most expensive detergent doesn't mean it's the best.

The best product to purchase would be a multi-purpose detergent. While liquid detergents target oil or grease stains, powder detergents are great for sand and other clay stains (Leverette, 2021).

Finding a multi-purpose cleaner can make each laundry load effective while saving you the cost of buying various detergents for different purposes. Tip: I recommend starting with a detergent pod. You can chuck them into the back of the washing machine with the clothes - easy! If you have sensitive skin, try a non-biological detergent. Buy a separate softener. It makes everything smell great, protects the fibers, and makes the items soft.

**Stains**

Ever wondered about stains and how you would treat them? You may have thought that some stains are meant to stick with you for life, but that is just not the case. With patience and care, you can treat a stain and remove it altogether.

For example, oil stains can be immediately covered with baby powder or cornstarch, left for a while, and then washed as normal. The powder will lift the oil and prevent the stain. Red wine stains can be covered with salt or baking soda and left for a while. Use dish soap, white vinegar, and warm water to remove coffee stains. Use toothpaste with aggressive rubbing to remove ink stains (Mark, 2021).

## Hand Wash Vs. Machine Wash

The days of hand washing clothes are almost entirely behind us. With machines even having a delicate hand wash option, there is no reason for us to physically or metaphorically get our hands dirty (or clean). But even machine washing is not as straightforward as tossing the clothes into the machine, with random amounts of detergents, and hoping for the best.

My first piece of advice would be to read the instructions and know what all the settings are on your washing machine before you use it for the first time. Once you know what every knob, button, and dial means, you can work on sorting your clothes. Sort into colors, whites, and delicate and normal items, and wash them accordingly. Remember, colors run, and you don't want your white clothes turning pink or any other type of strange and uneven color. Also, feel the texture of denim and lace or silk—they feel very different, with one feeling harder and the other texture feeling much softer and delicate. These can't be washed together, or the delicate items will fray or get damaged.

Although almost all machines have a setting to hand wash or wash delicate items, no machine can replicate the real deal. You may wonder how you would know what items should be washed by hand and what items are acceptable to go into the machine on a delicate cycle. Firstly, delicate items such as lingerie or other intimate garments will need to be hand-washed, and most silk items will need to be hand-washed. Wool sweaters or jerseys that tend to have a bit of a stretch should be hand-washed. Secondly, you may wonder why the machine is not good enough for these items. Well, in simple terms, a machine still twists and tosses items around, no matter how gentle. This causes the garments to stretch and lose their shape.

When you hand wash items, wash them gently, soaking them in detergent and gently rinsing them. Then use a softener, just a little in fresh warm water. You will feel the fabric become softer. Move the material around in the water, squeezing it gently, then carefully rinse again. Be careful not to wring them out too vigorously, or else you may end up with the same problem you may have with using a machine. If the item is stretchy, like a sweater, find somewhere you can lie it flat to dry and adjust it back into its original shape.

**Reading Clothing Labels**

Understanding clothing labels can feel a bit like trying to understand hieroglyphics. Those tiny symbols can be overwhelming, and reading them can leave you feeling like you will damage any clothing item.

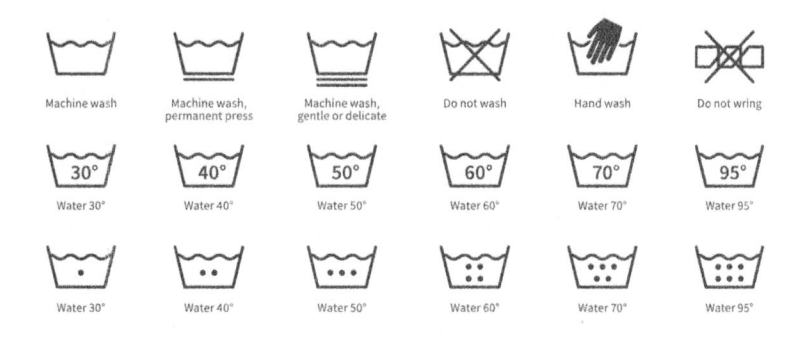

| Symbol | Meaning |
|---|---|
| Machine wash | Machine wash |
| Machine wash, permanent press | Machine wash, permanent press |
| Machine wash, gentle or delicate | Machine wash, gentle or delicate |
| Do not wash | Do not wash |
| Hand wash | Hand wash |
| Do not wring | Do not wring |
| Water 30° | Water 30° |
| Water 40° | Water 40° |
| Water 50° | Water 50° |
| Water 60° | Water 60° |
| Water 70° | Water 70° |
| Water 95° | Water 95° |
| Water 30° | Water 30° |
| Water 40° | Water 40° |
| Water 50° | Water 50° |
| Water 60° | Water 60° |
| Water 70° | Water 70° |
| Water 95° | Water 95° |

The symbol that looks like a bucket of water tells you whether a garment is; machine washable, the ideal temperature for washing, if it should be hand washed (displayed with a hand in the bucket), and whether it should be wrung or not.

Next, the label will tell you whether a clothing item can be bleached.

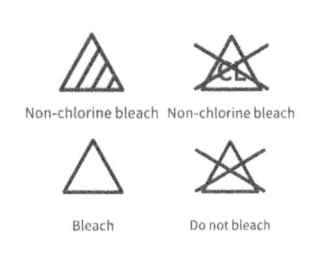

Ideally, colors should not be bleached because the bleach can cause the colors to fade. Bleaching is usually reserved for whites that have gotten dull and need some brightening. The bleach symbol is represented by a triangle.

| Symbol | Meaning |
|---|---|
| Non-chlorine bleach | Non-chlorine bleach |
| Non-chlorine bleach | Non-chlorine bleach |
| Bleach | Bleach |
| Do not bleach | Do not bleach |

KEEPING YOUR HOME CLEAN—THE TOOLS YOU NEED ... | 75

The square symbol with a circle tells you whether a clothing item can be tumbled-dried.

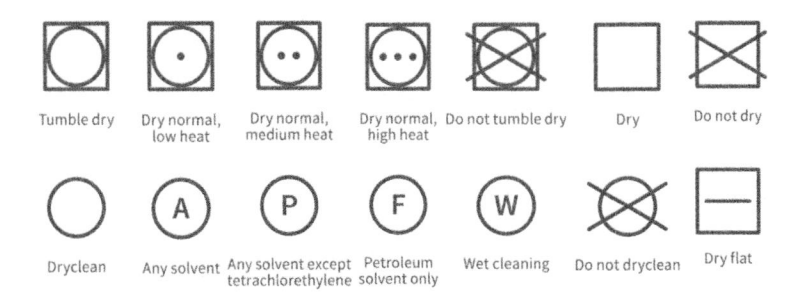

| Tumble dry | Dry normal, low heat | Dry normal, medium heat | Dry normal, high heat | Do not tumble dry | Dry | Do not dry |
| Dryclean | Any solvent | Any solvent except tetrachlorethylene | Petroleum solvent only | Wet cleaning | Do not dryclean | Dry flat |

And lastly, the little symbol that looks like an iron? Yes, you guessed it! It tells you whether you should iron the garment.

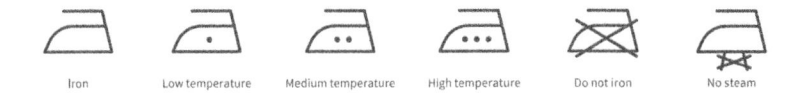

| Iron | Low temperature | Medium temperature | High temperature | Do not iron | No steam |

Whether or not it is suited to be ironed with a hot, medium, or cool iron, depends on the number of dots in the iron symbol. If a hot iron should be used, it will have three dots; if a medium iron should be used, it will have two dots; and if it only has one dot, you should use a cool iron (Ariel, n.d.).

**Becoming "Ironing" Man**

Ironing is often a high-stakes game. It is time-consuming; it has to be done right, and if you make one wrong move, you could destroy a perfectly good outfit. The first question I had when I was out on my own was, "Does this need to be ironed?" Now, the answer depends on multiple factors.

Firstly, suppose you have hung your clothes to dry in the fresh air. In that case, I recommend ironing them because little bugs can get caught in your clothes and could leave some nasty bites behind after you have worn them. Also, the sun tends to harden clothes, towels, and linens when left out to dry. Taking an iron to your clothes will help soften them up a bit.

Soft cotton items may also need ironing, mainly because they easily crease. But we are busy people and only want to spend time ironing the essentials. So a general rule of thumb is that you should iron formal wear and clothes that work as a top layer, i.e., the layer that the world sees.

Jeans don't necessarily need to be ironed. But shirts would need to be. There are also items of clothing that are intentionally wrinkled or meant to be wrinkled, you know, for fashion. You would follow the instructions on these items about ringing them out and leaving them to set in the correct shape.

To iron your clothes successfully, you will need some tools, the first and most important of which is an iron.

Next, you would need an ironing board. This is flat and firm, giving you the perfect surface to finish the job quickly and professionally. An ironing cloth can be handy. This cloth can be used over clothes with prints or beads and other delicate decals; after all, you wouldn't want to melt anything on your clothes.

Ironing is relatively straightforward, but it is something that you get better at over time. Watching wrinkles quickly vanish before your eyes can also be highly satisfying. Tip: To iron a shirt or blouse, best start with it when it is still slightly damp (no need for steam). Start with the collar, then the front top of the shirt just under the collar, the cuffs, then the back of the shirt at the top - just under the collar, it's called the yolk. Then the sleeves, the front main panels, and the back. Put it on a hanger and let it air off.

**Folding Laundry**

This is something that takes a while to get the hang of, and for a long time, my closet looked more like a dumping ground than it did a closet. That's because folding clothes and keeping them folded takes a lot of attention. It is a habit that forms over time, but it's a habit, nonetheless.

A great space-saving way of folding clothes is using the Marie Kondo method.

You'll start by laying a t-shirt flat on its front. Then you will fold one side until it meets the center and fold the sleeve back on itself. Do the same for the other side, then fold it in half lengthwise twice. This will give you a standard-size clothing item that can be packed in drawers or cupboards, allowing you to see all your folded items all the time (Picard, 2020).

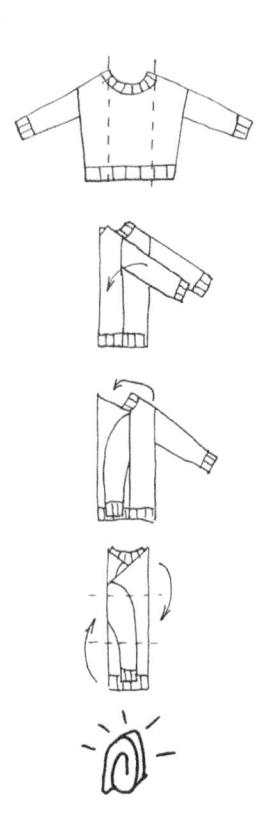

## Sewing and Mending

Ripped jeans are now a fashion statement. If you can think back on some torn or ripped clothing items, you just had to throw them away because they were unsalvageable. Well, that is not always the case. Yes, you can use your discretion about what can be repaired and what can't, but there are some clothing items that a needle and thread can restore to their former glory.

Similarly, you can always fix a button that has come loose and fallen off a shirt or blouse. All you need to do is thread the cotton through the needle's eye. Then thread it in one hole and out the next of the button while fixing (holding) it firmly to its desired place (so the needle goes all the way through the shirt material). Repeat this a few times, then with the two loose cotton ends on the inside of the shirt, tie them in a knot and trim off the ends with scissors. There are other ways of finishing the loose ends, but a knot will serve you well. Note: Be sure to line the button up perfectly with its corresponding hole before starting, and ensure you don't get your fingers in the way.

# ESSENTIAL HOME MAINTENANCE, CHECKS, AND SECURITY ENHANCEMENTS

*A*s intimidating as it may seem, finding your home and apartment isn't a one-and-done deal. Once you move in, you agree to a relationship of maintenance, ensuring your home stays up to scratch and livable at all times. This is not to deter you from moving out of your family home. Instead, it is to help you prepare for anything and everything you may face once you move out.

While homes don't take care of themselves, you can do a lot of home maintenance and preventative care by yourself; without the need to "call in an expert" and pay a call-out fee.

# ESSENTIAL HOME MAINTENANCE, CHECKS, AND SEC... | 81

I'm sure you've heard that prevention is better than cure. Well, believe it or not, the same thing goes for your home maintenance. Think of it this way: you'd instead fix the leaky faucet in your bathroom, so you don't have to call a plumber at 2:00 a.m. with a gushing tap that refuses to close. You'd have to turn off the water at the mains and hope the plumber comes before someone needs to use and flush the toilet. Fixing the faulty washer before it becomes a disaster will save you a lot of cash in the long run. But it doesn't just apply to leaky taps. There are many things that you can fix up quickly at home as soon as you notice them. It may save you from making a large insurance claim (yes, you do need insurance, it is not a scam) or losing the value of your home.

## WHEN TO INSPECT YOUR HOME

Don't get me wrong, you don't need to pull out a hard hat and a checklist and set an entire day aside to go through every nook and cranny of your home. There are things you'd be able to check as you go about your day, and eventually, you become so accustomed to checking it that it doesn't seem like much of a chore. For example, suppose you notice that your monthly water bill is higher than usual. In that case, you might check if any faucets are leaking. Some things are easier to check than others, like a lightbulb that has fused. The darkness will alert you that the lightbulb is no longer functioning. But some things need to be physically checked, like your fire alarms, which must be checked quite often.

## BOILER MAINTENANCE CHECKS

Boilers are great. They keep our homes and water warm and are usually neatly tucked away somewhere in our homes. But this usually means they are out of sight and out of mind. It is highly recommended that boilers be serviced and inspected once a year to ensure it functions and operates optimally and that you don't have to increase the internal pressure (Campion, 2022).

Regular maintenance on your boiler will minimize your risk of a breakdown and allow your boiler to have a longer lifespan. Boilers can become dangerous if left uninspected and maintained. Please get licensed experts to do this for you. Tip: You should get a copy of the boiler certificate with your rental agreement. You can see when it was last serviced. You want evidence that it has been regularly maintained and that the certificate is still in date. The tradesperson's name or company may be on the certificate. If you want to use them for the next service, you can just contact them directly.

There are other warning signs that you can look out for in your boiler. If it makes too much noise, it could be because of air in your boiler, low pressure, or a buildup of sludge. Your boiler may make some noise, but it is worth getting it checked if it is excessive and very loud. Also, if you find that your boiler is leaking, it could be because of a leaking pump, incorrectly installed pipework, or worse, corrosion which would mean that you'd need to install a new one (SSE, n.d.).

GUTTERS

I know; you've probably even forgotten that you have gutters. Still, every year, without fail, the rainy season rolls around. Your home's gutter system serves an integral role in rainwater drainage. The rainwater that falls on your home's roof is drained through the gutters and downpipes. Suppose your gutters are blocked, backed up, or damaged. In that case, you could find yourself facing water damage to your roof and even causing a leaky ceiling as the rainwater stands for long periods on your roof. If the drainage of your gutter isn't effective, you could even have water seeping into your walls.

It is recommended that you clean your gutters out twice a year. This will minimize a buildup that negatively impacts your home's water drainage. If your house is surrounded by trees, you have a lot of leaves that fall onto the roof, and you live in an area that experiences heavy rainfall. You will need to clean your gutters up to three times a year.

There are a few ways that you could clean your gutter. The first would be to make a hefty investment in gutter-cleaning equipment. Still, you are probably looking for cost-effective solutions. The second method would be to hire someone to step in and clean your gutter for you. But once again, we are looking for a cost-effective solution. The best solution is to get a ladder. Make sure it is safe, secure, and has sufficient height to reach your gutters safely. Then, with a pair of gloves, you can clean out the debris, leaves, and dirt that has built up in your gutters. Be sure to have a bag or a bucket that is easy enough to carry safely to the top of the ladder so that you can put all the leaves and dirt into that bag or bucket. After that, it should be easy enough for you to dispose of (Edwards, n.d.).

AIR VENTS

If you have them in your home, just thinking about dirty air vents may make you scrunch your nose and fight back a sneeze. Air vents are most commonly found in US houses and modern homes in the UK. If left uncleaned for long periods, your air vents build up extreme amounts of dust, dirt, pollen, insects, and other things that make your nose tingle and your eyes puffy. While it is usually suggested that you clean your air vents every two to three years, you should clean them out more often if you have kids or pets.

Now let's get to the good part. There are two ways that you can clean your air vents, both of which involve a vacuum cleaner. First, if you are moving into a new home and don't know when the vents were last cleaned, or if you unscrew the vents and are met with a horrific, dusty sight. You may want to do a deep clean, which may involve hiring a heavy-duty vacuum cleaner. Alternatively, use your regular vacuum, but clean it more frequently, so the buildup doesn't reach DEFCON 1.

To clean the air vents, you will unscrew the vent covers. Give those a clean, too, because they come off the vent entirely. You can wash them down with warm soapy water in the sink. But be careful not to lose any screws. Next, you will turn your vacuum on and place it in the air vent. Using a standard home vacuum cleaner, you would snake the nozzle into the vent as far as possible while wiggling the nozzle around to cover as much surface area as possible.

You want to make sure that you peek inside and get a good look to ensure that all dust, mold, and everything else has been effectively cleaned. If you're struggling to get a decent look inside, snap a few pics with your camera phone.

## RADIATORS

As it heads into winter, you may also want to check that your radiators work in tip-top shape. When you turn the radiator on, you might feel that it is cold at the top and warm at the bottom. It may also be making bubbling noises; chances are that there is air trapped you need to bleed out.

When you bleed the radiator, it would need to be entirely cooled down; we don't want anyone burnt with hot water.

You can get a bleed key that fits the valve, and you would turn it counterclockwise to open the valve and clockwise to close it. Open the bleed valve, usually located at the top of the radiator, and wait for a hissing sound. When you hear the sound, that is how you will know that the air has been released. Having a cloth or towel on hand is a good idea to catch any water that may very well squirt from the valve. Be sure to lay a rag on the floor to catch any drips and so you don't slip on a wet floor.

Once the hissing sound stops, you can close your valve, and your radiator should be good to go.

## DRAINS

Another thing that always seems to cause some sort of problem in every home are drains. They are always blocked and clogged, but these are blockages that happen with use. If you find a clogged drain, you don't need to call in a plumber every time.

Instead, a plunger is the most important tool you will need in your artillery. There are two types of plungers, one for sinks and the other for toilets.

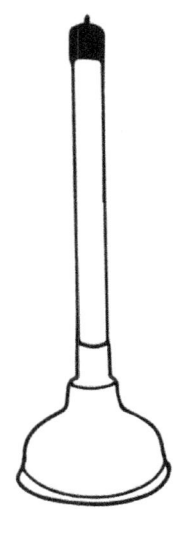

The way to know that there is a blockage in the drain is to see which sinks and toilets are slow to drain. It is there where you are going to use the plunger. Forming a firm suction against the drain's opening, you will plunge two or three times until the drainage clears. You will also need to ensure that you have a bag to dispose of the dislodged blockage.

There are also other ways of clearing blockages; using a drain snake, pouring boiling water down the drain, using a liquid drain unblocker from your local store, or calling in a professional. This can mostly be avoided if you regularly maintain your plumbing and dislodge any blockages as and when they appear.

There are a few things that you can do to prevent a blockage from forming, such as putting a drain screen over all drains so no strange items flow down into the pipes. You also must ensure that you never throw any cooking grease or cooking oil down the drain. This will cause clogs and leave you with strange odors around your home. To prevent a blocked toilet, I suggest buying a cheaper two-ply toilet paper rather than a quilted thick toilet paper. Cheaper toilet paper is usually thinner and gets broken down by the water much faster. You won't have a blocked toilet as often and may save money.

Your home's plumbing is also an area you never want to neglect. Once you invest in a plunger, you are all set for small challenges, but you can treat your drains every three to six months with an enzyme or powder drain cleaner. You can speak to someone at your local hardware store to get a product that helps prevent blockages. Note: preventatively using products meant for more heavy-duty blockages could erode your pipes if used too often.

You can also keep your drains smelling great by throwing a few drops of essential oil into the drain each night.

## TURNING OFF YOUR WATER SUPPLY

Suppose you have a persistent leak in your bathroom or even your toilet. Before you can work on or repair it, you will need to turn off the main water supply. This is the case whether fixing the leak or calling in a professional.

There are two ways to shut off the water supply. First, you can shut off a localized water supply which is water being supplied to a specific outlet such as a toilet or your washing machine. These usually look like taps that aren't connected to a faucet. You can turn that off to fix a localized water problem. But if you have a burst pipe or a leaky roof, you must turn off your water at the main supply. Usually, located on the outside wall of your home and will have clear markings on which way to close and open the supply. Once all the repair work has been done, you can turn on the water supply, which will also help you ensure that the leak has been entirely fixed.

## TRIPPED CIRCUIT BREAKER

Nothing is more annoying than turning on the hairdryer and suddenly, the power goes out. When this happens, I usually open the curtains to peek outside and see if it is just me or if the entire neighborhood is out.

It's even more nerve-wracking to realize that only your lights are out. This probably means that your circuit has tripped. Many causes will lead to a tripped circuit. There could be too many appliances in use or too many things drawing electricity which overloads the circuit. Something could be causing interference, which could lead to electrical damage or fire (for example, a connected appliance coming into contact with water). Whatever it may be, having your circuit break is usually good as it is an instant safety mechanism.

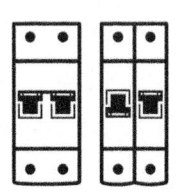

To turn the power back on, you would need to locate the main circuit board of your home. It can usually be found in the basement, garage, or even in the passageway of your home. You will see that the main switch or a specific switch may be off (tripped) or in the mid-way position. Before turning it back on, you will want to ensure that all appliances plugged into this specific circuit are turned off. If you were using the hair dryer or the kettle when the lights tripped, immediately disconnect that appliance and others connected to the circuit. If the switch is midway, flip it all the way so that it is completely off, and then you can flip the switch back on. You can check the lights or an appliance on that circuit to ensure power has been restored. Be careful when using too many appliances in one go. If the lights go out when it's dark, you will do the same thing. Make sure you have a flashlight on hand—I like to store my flashlight near my main switch (Wallender, 2022).

## HANGING A PICTURE

So now that you're in your new place, you may want to make it feel a little more like home. This includes hanging some paintings and pictures and making everything feel more like your own space. If you're wondering how to hang items on your wall, there are two ways: using nails that are more permanent or using methods without nails.

To hang pictures and paintings on the wall with nails, you would first need to make sure that you have nails that are large and strong enough to hold the weight of the picture you are hoping to hang, and you would need to have a hammer. Then you need to ensure that the holes or hooks on the picture that will hang onto the nails are perfectly lined up and marked so that you knock the nail into the right place. There are many ways to do this, such as using a marker and ruler and taking accurate measurements. Or you could place a small amount of toothpaste into the holes on the frame, place the frame on the wall, and the toothpaste will leave a mark for where you need to knock the nails in. Holding the nail in place, perpendicular to the wall, you'll start with slow and minor knocks with the hammer, being extremely careful not to knock your finger. Once you have tapped the nail a few times and it is secure, you will remove your fingers and knock it in entirely until there is half an inch or one centimeter of the nail sticking out. There should be just enough space to hang your picture on the nail.

Tip: If the plaster on the walls of your home is too old, it is likely to crumble if you hit a nail on it. Instead, the better option would be to use a drill if you have one and drill a hole at the height you want to hang the picture. Use a wall plug or an anchor and insert it into the wall, then use a screw instead of a nail to hang the picture. Ensure that the head of the screw you use isn't too big for the hook or hole in your picture.

ESSENTIAL HOME MAINTENANCE, CHECKS, AND SEC... | 93

If you want to hang a picture without nails and use two-way tape or adhesives, the toothpaste trick may hinder the adhesive properties of the two-way tape. The best way, in this case, would be to use the measuring tape and marker trick. Then, follow the instructions that come with the adhesive you will be using. Some instructions may differ from product to product, and some products may not be able to hold heavier frames. All of this needs to be taken into account before hanging your pictures. For example, some adhesives may require a flat surface to adhere to. Others may require you not to have painted the wall for seven days. And others may require time to set, which could vary from half an hour to three hours. Be sure to read all instructions carefully.

HOW TO PUT UP A SHELF

While also making your home feel more like home, you may decide to decorate and put up some shelving for various reasons. You may go shopping for a shelf, see a beautiful one, and buy it, only to come home and realize that it has to be constructed from scratch.

Depending on the shelf you get, you may need to screw in brackets, each of which will vary depending on the shelf you are using and the weight you plan to place on the shelf. Generally, when you are installing shelves or constructing shelving, there will be detailed instructions that come in the packaging. You are required to use these as they will show you how to build and install your shelves and be safe.

You may need screwdrivers on hand, drills to drill holes for wall plugs, and screws to hang the shelves up, but in most cases, the screws and wall plugs will be included in the packaging. The packaging may also contain allen keys and other small bits and bobs you need. Keep all the little tools in the packaging. If you ever need to deconstruct your furniture, say if you move or for any other reason, they will come in handy.

Also, don't be frightened of hardware stores. The screws and wall plugs included in the package are not always the best solution for every wall. Your walls might need slightly bigger, more robust wall plugs and screws. If you know this to be the case, head into the hardware store, and you will find that there is usually someone in the store who can help you choose the best items for you.

## PATCHING A HOLE

So, you've hung up a picture, and now you need to take it down for some reason. Whatever the reason, we sometimes find ourselves with holes in our drywall or

ESSENTIAL HOME MAINTENANCE, CHECKS, AND SEC... | 95

our plastered wall. While this may not pose any structural problems, it is a sore sight to behold and should probably be repaired as soon as possible. Depending on the size of the hole you face, you can use a drywall patch to cover the area and firmly cover it with spackle or filler applied with a putty knife. This is the best method of repairing a wall.

When you start your repair, you must ensure that you have protective gloves and goggles, so no paint chips get into your eyes. You can then prep the wall surface and paste your spackle or filler with the putty knife onto the wall in a similar way that you'd place butter on toast. Make sure all the edges are smooth, and it does not look lumpy or bumpy. Once the spackle or filler has dried, you will go in with some fine sandpaper to ensure that everything is smooth and flat. You may need to repeat these steps if, when sanded, there is still a tiny hole or two. Tip: Wrap the fine sandpaper around a wooden block or something else perfectly flat. It will give it a professional, smooth finish. You can then prime and paint the repaired patch, and if you do a good job, you will never even know that a hole once existed in that spot.

## SQUEAKY HINGES

Having squeaky hinges can be quite unsettling if you find yourself alone in a brand-new home. Luckily, there are quite a few ways to remedy the squeaks without needing to buy any specialized products. Products such as WD-40, silicone spray, or lithium grease work great on squeaky hinges. Still, products around your home can work just as well. The best way to stop a squeaky hinge is to lubricate it. Try spraying hairspray onto the hinge, applying olive oil using a syringe to the hinge to ensure it gets into all the grooves and crevices or using a dry bar of soap. Swing the door back and forth a few times to let the hairspray, oil, or soap work its way into the hinge. You could also use petroleum jelly or wax candles to eliminate the squeak. Still, you may need to remove the hinge pin and coat it with petroleum jelly or wax.

## LOST KEYS

If you find yourself without your keys when you need them most, there may be some tips and tricks you can use to get back into your home or into your car if you are locked out. The first thing you would need to do is ensure that you have a spare set of keys. I like to have an extra set that I can leave with someone I trust, for example, parents or friends. So when I am stuck, I can always get back in.

Next, you can download key-finding apps that allow you to pinpoint the location of your keys using Bluetooth transmission. However, the best way of keeping track of your keys at home is to have a designated space in your home where you can keep them. This could be a key hanger, a box, or a small basket. So you never have to run around the house looking for them. Tips:

1. Keep your key location discrete.
2. Do not keep your keys next to the front or back door. If you get a break-in, don't make it easy for thieves to open all your doors. It gives them easy access to remove your belongings and drive away in your car!

Suppose you find yourself in a situation where you are locked outside your home with no alternative. In that case, having a local locksmith's number on hand is always good. If you are in a new area and are unfamiliar with your neighbors, Google will be a great help.

## KEEPING DOCUMENTS SAFE

Where is your birth certificate? Where is your passport? If your heart suddenly leaped into your throat, perhaps you should find those immediately! Some of the most valuable things in our possession are not jewelry or money but essential documents. You need to keep documents safe: your birth certificate, identity documents or social security cards, tax returns and financial statements, insurance documents, and your last will and testament.

You could keep these documents in a filing cabinet, a plastic sleeve in a lockable closet, or a safety deposit box. I prefer to keep all important documentation together in the same place, so I am not searching high and low in different places for different documents.

It is essential to keep these documents safe in case of emergency. You would need to be able to tell someone where they can find all documentation that may be necessary for specific emergencies. Also, keeping these documents safe means minimizing the risk of becoming a victim of identity theft and fraud.

## CYBER AND PHYSICAL SECURITY

We live in an unsafe world. A world where you need to be street-smart to survive because there are predators of all kinds lurking behind every corner. It goes without saying that you must ensure you are always safe and secure, both digitally and physically.

**Phone Security: Preventing Theft/Loss**

You must ensure that your phone is safe and easy to locate. You can activate the "Find My Device" feature on your phone to search for it from another device when it has been misplaced. Make sure you have a password lock on your phone and that all your data is backed up. Also, it goes without saying that you should never leave your phone in the line of temptation. Avoid leaving it in your car or visible to strangers, such as in an open bag or your back pocket.

If your data is backed up, you can make sure that you don't lose access to valuable information, and you can erase your device remotely.

**Home Network and Wi-Fi**

You must ensure that your home network and Wi-Fi are safe and secure. People don't need to be in your home to access it. Also, with the amount of sensitive data that passes through your home network, you need to ensure that it doesn't get hacked and the security isn't compromised.

**Antivirus and Firewalls**

It is essential to ensure that when downloading and installing software on your phone, computer, or any other device, ensure it is from a reputable company. Or else you may end up with a virus. It is also essential to ensure that you have a firewall installed in your browser and antivirus software on your devices. This ensures that nothing harmful can compromise your devices. It is always worth spending a bit of money and attention on ensuring your digital safety is up to scratch.

**Passwords and Two-Factor Authentication**

Having the same password for everything is not secure and having the same password for five years is not safe either. It is handy to have passwords saved. Today we use passwords for everything. You can save them virtually or write them down in a journal (if you do write them down, ensure they are kept in a safe and secure place). Please change your passwords often and ensure that it is never something simple or easy enough for anyone to guess. Examples include; password, qwerty, 12345, monkey, Your Name, etc.

ESSENTIAL HOME MAINTENANCE, CHECKS, AND SEC... | 101

Two-factor authentication adds an extra level of security when accessing applications. This is done by recognizing the device you often use to access these same applications. If a new device tries to access the app, you will be notified, and you can confirm or deny access.

**On The Web**

When you are surfing the web and you are online, you should always make sure that you are using an updated browser so that you aren't faced with glitches. Don't enter any personal information and banking information into browsers. You could become a victim of cyber fraud.

**Phishing**

STOP! DO NOT click on any foreign links! Whether sent to you via email or through any other methods. Fraudsters use links to lure you into clicking them, ultimately gaining access to your private information. When you see a message from your bank, you will want to ensure everything is good, especially when you see an error alert popping up on a text or email. Your bank will never ask you to click on a link, so always be sure to call your bank and report such emails or texts. That's what these fraudsters do—they put out a line in the form of a link, and they hope that someone is gullible enough to bite.

If you have been caught in a scam, alert your bank if money has been accessed; they will block and freeze any transactions until the problem can be resolved. If you find you have been hacked, change your passwords immediately. And lastly, make sure you are familiar with some of the ways that you can report fraud or cybercrime to authorities. Remember to trust your gut instinct. If you are in the slightest suspicious about something, chances are you need to be cautious.

**Talking to Strangers**

The rule of not talking to strangers is something that should stay in effect all through your life. Whether online or over the phone, do not give out private and personal information. Do not reveal your exact location. Do not send images of yourself or your family members to strangers. If someone makes you uncomfortable with unwanted sexual advances, report it immediately! Chances are they are also doing this to others.

**Home Security**

When you move into a new place, you want to ensure that when you lay your head down at night, your safety and security are not a concern. Yes, it is scary to think of crime, and it is a reality in modern times, but ideally, you don't want to sleep with one eye open at any given time. You can make some considerations regarding safety before and after you move in.

When looking at a possible apartment or house, we always look for things like mold or rust, and we forget the safety element. Instead, pay attention to little things. Research the safety and security of the neighborhood before moving in. Whether on Google, local community forums, or knocking on doors and asking residents what the crime is like in the area.

Next, you will want to check the lighting in and around your potential home. Are the hallways and parking areas lit? Can someone see you, and can you quickly see someone else? Ensure you check the lighting with someone during the night because the lighting is integral to security.

You will also need to check the doors and windows of your new potential home. What is the locking system like? Are there locks and deadbolts on the door? Is there a peephole, do the windows lock, and if not, would you be able to enhance these locking mechanisms? When checking the entrances and exits to the apartment, check the emergency exits of the building. It is often something that gets left unnoticed.

Once you move in, you can then increase and enhance your security. While this won't change the whole neighborhood, it will hopefully do a good enough job of ensuring that the already safe neighborhood is made much safer.

You may not always be able to do so when you're renting, but change the locks on all the doors and windows if you can. You can even keep the old locks in a safe place to replace them once your lease is up or you decide to move. You can also install a security system in your apartment with an armed response or an alarm alert - if you feel the area warrants this.

Next, you want to make sure you meet your neighbors and know who to call if you find yourself in a pickle. Cover your windows with curtains and get a door jammer to ensure your nights are much more peaceful.

Lastly, you can invest in other security components like cameras that connect to your mobile device through a wireless connection.

Always ensure safety is a top priority regardless of where you are and where life leads you. You deserve to be safe.

# ESSENTIAL INFO YOU NEED FOR RENTING

*R*enting a home is not always easy. You don't just pick a random property, sign the papers, and unpack your belongings. Instead, it takes a lot of hard work and consideration. There are so many things to consider, and the chances of you finding your dream apartment are not all that high. Maybe you won't get a walk-in closet and an ensuite bathroom. Perhaps you won't get the large kitchen with the eye-level oven. You may need to compromise on some things, especially with budgets and other factors that need to be considered. You need to understand what is in your budget range for renting because rent money is not the only expense you will have. It would be best if you also considered where you are moving to. If you leave your home country, the cost of living elsewhere will be different from where you currently live. This means you must learn how to budget in another country and possibly another currency.

**Renting Guide**

Renting is great when you aren't looking for a long-term commitment. This works well if you are moving out of the nest for the first time to head off to college or to start your first job. Renting, in the short term, is more cost-effective than buying. But that does not mean it is cheap, especially if you are looking for something neat, safe, and comfortable. Here is a step-by-step breakdown of everything you need to do to ensure you are getting the best deal.

PLAN YOUR BUDGET

Don't move to a new city for a job you don't yet have. When you get a job, you will probably know your salary and how much you will earn weekly, monthly, and annually. This will help you with your budget plans to find an affordable place. While keeping considerations such as groceries, cars, and other expenses within your budget.

Remember that rent money is just one financial aspect of finding a home. You'd need to look closely at your lease agreement to know if you have to pay for any utilities on your own, which is often the case. Is there a monthly fee you must pay the landlord for maintenance and upkeep? Is there a communal pool, gym, or garden you would be required to contribute towards? Many other costs over and above your rent need to be considered. Be careful not to overlook those as you may find yourself quickly drowning financially.

## MAKE A CRITERIA

While you may have to compromise on some aspects of the home you're looking for, it is always good to have a list of things you are looking for. Never go into a place blind or without some idea of what you want or need in a home. You may find yourself paying a hefty rental in an area that doesn't even have half of what you need.

If you're more of a bath person than a shower person, you'd need to look for a place with a bathtub. If you are hoping for a two-bedroom with a separate guest bathroom, make a note of that. Small things often get overlooked, but if you have them written down, you'll know and remember what you need. Tip: Location is critical. This should be very high on your criteria list. The right area can make all the difference in making you love your new place. It's better to prioritize a safe, great location over an extra bathroom or some added extra you don't really need.

## YOU AND YOUR LANDLORD

Before moving into an apartment, to ensure that your renting experience is as pleasant as possible, you must know the duties, expectations, and responsibilities of you and your landlord. This will be detailed in your lease agreement, and problems that cannot be resolved may be escalated to higher authorities. For example, your landlord is required to carry out any maintenance or repairs in your apartment. Still, you may be liable for the cost of such repairs. If you had a party that got out of hand, your friend might have hammered a huge hole in the wall. The landlord can call someone in to repair it or repair it themselves, but you will be responsible for the cost.

Law requires landlords to ensure that homes and apartments are habitable. They need to make sure that they are safe, and they are required to present you with compliance certificates with your lease agreement. This will ensure that there are no gas leaks, no electrical faults, no water damage, and that no mold is growing around the house. Before you call in your own plumber or repairman, you need to liaise and communicate with your landlord first.

## EXTENDING OR ENDING LEASE/TENANCY

It is always good to have some forethought when moving into a rental property. Your decision to stay in a place will change when you move in. Maybe you have noisy neighbors and need to get out of there, or perhaps you love it and want to stay there for at least five years.

When you start renting, make sure you know what your lease agreement says about extending your tenancy before your lease agreement expires. Lease agreements are usually set for a year. If the landlord or the rental agency knows your lease ends a year from now, they may start marketing your apartment in 10 months. If you plan on extending your tenancy, you will need to see how many months' notice you would need to provide, and you would need to inform them of how long you are hoping to extend your stay.

Because some leases are set for one year, you may lose out on an entire month's rent or more if you want to end your lease early. This is a penalty for not staying for the whole of the agreed-upon time. This is also why the first and last month's rent is required when your lease agreement is signed. Be sure to read all the fine print and know precisely what is needed from you if you want to extend your stay or cut it short.

## DOCUMENTS TO KEEP

Whether you are renting in a different town or another country, there are essential things you would need for your lease agreement to be successful. You would need your passport, proof of employment or a letter from your employer, financial information such as a bank statement or a letter from your bank, your social security number or identity documents, and a letter from your previous landlord.

## THE COST OF RENTING

The cost will vary greatly depending on where you stay and your apartment type. Suppose you are renting a one-bedroom bachelor apartment. In that case, it will probably be cheaper than a three-bedroom, two-bathroom, or penthouse apartment.

To give you a rough idea of price, from statistics collected worldwide. Data is compiled from the most expensive one-bedroom apartments in city centers down to the cheapest, depending on the city. For example, in US dollars, a one-bedroom apartment in the city center of Singapore is around $2,314.17 per month (NUMBEO, n.d.). This is the most expensive rental rate globally. In comparison, a one-bedroom apartment in the city center of the US would cost around $1,679.23

ESSENTIAL INFO YOU NEED FOR RENTING | 111

per month. In Canada, it would cost $1,183.73 per month, and in the UK, it would cost $1,008.38 per month (NUMBEO, n.d.).

Living outside the city in a suburb could also be a viable option. Just make sure you factor in the increase in your monthly travel costs. Otherwise, it could actually cost you more!

**Security Deposit**

A security deposit is charged by the landlord or the rental agency to make sure that you have some financial incentive to keep the rental property in the best shape possible. With the threat of financial loss (your security deposit), landlords and rental agencies know that you will not purposefully destroy the apartment in which you are living.

If the apartment is found to be in the same condition that you received it in, you may get your deposit back.

As a tip, take photos of any defects when you first move into a place. Send a copy to the landlord and keep your copy safe. You don't want to be held responsible and pay for someone else's mishaps or damage.

A security deposit is paid when you take occupancy of your rented space, usually between one and one and a half months' rent. This cost can be higher if you have other risks like pets. Therefore, you may pay a higher security deposit to cover the cost of a carpet or furniture that your pet may damage.

In most cases, if there has been unavoidable damage to your apartment, such as chipped paint or a stain on the carpet, landlords may deduct the cost of cleaning or repair from your security deposit. You may get something back despite the damage that was caused. However, this will need to be checked in your lease agreement. Some landlords and rental agencies may keep the entire security deposit for any damages incurred.

It is also good to make sure you always have a good relationship with your landlord and not be the cause of any trouble in your apartment.

**Administration Fees**

Your landlord or rental agency will likely charge you an administration fee or application fee when you apply for and are given an apartment to rent.

**Moving Costs**

So now that you have decided on an apartment, you are ready to make the big move. You are getting boxes from your grocer and packing things, marking them as you go. You have your friends helping with the promise of pizza once everything is done.

In the thick of packing, hiring movers may have crossed your mind. But just like choosing your perfect apartment, it is not that straightforward. Movers can be costly, and the actual cost depends greatly on several variables. The first thing to consider when moving furniture is whether it is a short or long distance. Hiring movers for a short distance can cost between $800 to $2,150, and long-distance can cost anything between $2,200 and $5,700 (Perry, 2022). Depending on the furniture you are transporting and whether any items are fragile or specialty goods. There may be an additional cost. You also need to know what comes with your moving team. Often you will get two people and a truck to do your moving. This may cost extra if you have many or extremely heavy items requiring more movers and a truck with a tailgate (a lift at the back for unloading).

There are, however, alternatives that you could consider.

Hiring a moving truck and driving it yourself may be more cost-effective. All you will pay for is the rental of the truck, but you will need to make sure your friends are up to helping you do some heavy lifting. You will also need to put fuel into the truck as it may not come with a full tank. When you return the truck, it usually needs to be returned with fuel at the same level you received.

If this is your first move and you haven't acquired much furniture and don't have a whole home full of items to move, it makes sense to consider doing the move yourself. Do an assessment to see what oversized items you possess, ones that may not fit in your car. You can then see if you'd need to hire a trailer or a moving truck, and the rest of your items can be packed into your car. Some considerations would need to be made if you are moving far from home. Perhaps you can get help from friends and family to make the long-distance trip easier and more enjoyable.

**Renters Insurance**

You may also need to pay for renters (tenants) and contents insurance. The renter's insurance is split into two parts. First is insurance to cover the cost of accidental damage to any items belonging to the landlord they have provided for you to use listed in your agreement. The second covers other contents, such as all your belongings. The renter's (tenant's) insurance will protect the belongings. The landlord's insurance should cover, for example, damage to pipes and the actual building. But if you have not maintained the property and, for instance, damaged the pipes and caused a leak, this is your fault. You would be expected to pay for the plumber and the parts required. Your insurance would not usually cover this. If the damage is due to natural wear and tear, the landlord is responsible for getting those pipes fixed or replaced.

Your insurance will only go so far, depending on who is responsible for the damage. Your belongings should be covered if damaged by an accidental internal leak in your apartment or if they were stolen. It's worth noting that you need to read every line in your insurance document. Checking what is covered and what is not. Some insurance companies provide extra cover - such as the cost of getting out a plumber, but for an additional price. The cheapest insurance is not always the best. You want a company known for paying out claims timely and reliably. So pick a reputable, well-known company. Every insurance document is different, so know yours!

## Utilities and Bills

Now that you have the big move out of the way and spent your first month in your new home, your utility bill inevitably comes around. Whether you are pleasantly surprised or troubled by the bill, it needs to be paid. Your bill will include a variety of state or government-provided services. In the UK, your bills could consist of electricity, gas, water, and council tax which covers bin collections. In the US, it will include electricity, water, and gas.

For you not to get a surprise, asking your landlord for advice regarding the average utility bill in your apartment building may be worthwhile. Knowing how much you can expect to pay when the first month ends is always good.

It is always great to set automatic payments a day or two after your salary comes in to ensure you never miss or skip a payment. This will allow your utilities to be paid first, and you won't spend the money that has been earmarked for your bills. You can also adjust the date that your bills are due to coincide with payday, and you can set automatic reminders for a day or two before your bills are due. Suppose you don't want to touch the money you would have used to pay your utilities. In that case, creating a separate account for your automated payments may be a good idea.

**Other Costs**

It would be best to consider Wi-Fi options and your phone costs together. They may be part of your monthly expenses. Monthly subscriptions will need to be paid on time to avoid any penalties that you may incur. There may be cost savings if you get both services from one provider.

You may also have the added cost of having someone help you with cleaning and laundry in your home. Paying for a housekeeping service is great when you have a busy schedule and little time on weekends to do the chores. You would need to factor these costs into your budget, and often it may exclude cleaning supplies you would need to have on hand too.

COST SAVING STRATEGIES

There are ways to reduce utility costs by doing small things that add up. Little things like turning off a light when you leave the room or turning off the TV (on the wall) when you aren't watching are all ways to save. Consider switching to energy-saving light bulbs, unplugging all appliances that are not used, turning off the aircon or thermostat when you are not at home, and using natural ventilation, like opening windows to cool your home down (Becker, 2022). Also, depending on your energy supplier, electricity may be cheaper in the evening during off-peak hours. This is an excellent time to set your washing machine to start.

# 5

# PERSONAL CARE—TAKING CARE OF YOUR HAIR, SKIN, AND BODY

*B*eing out on your own, being independent, and exploring the world as your own person, not tethered to your parents, comes with finding a new version of yourself. While you may be nervous and scared to face the world as an adult, you sure don't have to look like it. Taking proper care of yourself, how you dress, your skin, and hair can give you more confidence and make you feel ready to take on the world.

## SKIN CARE

Taking care of your skin is essential for many reasons, not only to prevent skin diseases but also for aesthetic purposes. Also, it is a part of our bodies, and who doesn't want to keep their body healthy? Taking care of your skin is part of a healthy lifestyle, and by looking at your face, you will be reminded to take care of your body on the inside by hydrating. Your skin, your body's largest organ, sheds daily, meaning it may look different daily. It deserves all the care possible since it faces harsh environments. Following a detailed skincare routine is like giving your skin a big hug. It is worth your energy to invest in a routine that is suited to your skin. Everyone's skin is different, so whether you are consulting with professionals or seeing a dermatologist, it is worth getting a skincare routine that's best for you.

**Skin Care Routine**

Developing a routine is important. Your routine needs to follow some basic rules. Have a morning routine where you would include a sun protection step and a nighttime routine so you can go to sleep without makeup on. Before creating a skincare routine, there are other things that you would need to do to make your skin look its best. Stop eating junk and oily foods. Make sure you drink enough water. Don't sunbathe or spend too much time in the sun when it can be avoided. Remember that in your 20s and even in your 30s, you can still experience breakouts. You also want to make sure that you avoid touching your face and that if you do, your hands are clean. Lastly, remember that products in your hair can cause breakouts. If your hair is oily and is constantly touching your face, you may have to deal with acne or a rash.

The best skincare routine is one that happens once or twice a day. Remember that your skin produces its own natural oils, and you don't want to strip those oils away by washing too frequently.

In the morning, you want to apply a cleanser and clean your face and neck properly. Then you're going to move on to eye cream and a moisturizer, and lastly, you are going to apply sunscreen. Tip: Many modern moisturizers have sun protection, perfect for day wear. Check the packaging when you buy; it will save you time in your routine.

In the evening, especially if you have been wearing makeup all day, you need to cleanse your skin. Then you are going to use a toner and moisturizer before bed. This will allow your face to rejuvenate and feel much better after a day of exposure. Tip: Once or twice a week, exfoliate before cleansing in the evening. Some exfoliants can be abrasive, especially if used too frequently. If your skin is very sensitive, omit this step. Just do what suits your skin.

## HAIR CARE

Keeping your hair clean and healthy is essential for many reasons, one of which we have mentioned is keeping your skin healthy. But ensuring your hair is taken care of will prevent hair loss and make you feel good.

Depending on your hair texture, your hair care routine may vary. Treating curly hair may require you to add moisturizing products to your hair to hold the curl pattern without tangles and frizziness. Fine hair may need you to use extra heat protection, even when out in the sun, so your hair doesn't get sun damaged or to protect it from heated styling equipment. Find out what hair routine is best for you but avoid testing, experimenting, and spending lots of money on hair products. Try asking a family member with similar hair texture—how they treat their hair. You could also ask your hairdresser or barber, and they will give you tips on treating and styling your hair type.

Many hair care products are available on the market, so choosing the right ones can be tricky. Usually, you would select the products that best fit your hair type. And if you already have specific products you have been using, and they work for you, then there isn't a reason to change.

You shouldn't wash your hair too often as it may strip it of natural oils.

Lukewarm is better than hot water for washing your hair. Hot water can cause breakage and dryness. Too cold, and it won't be easy to get your scalp clean.

Avoid brushing longer hair when it is wet. This is when it is at its weakest, and it will snap. Also, cleaning your hairbrush at least once a week is vital, which we often forget to do.

**Cutting Your Hair**

You will usually trim your hair depending on a variety of factors. If you have short hair and you want to keep hair short, you may find yourself cutting your hair once a month or every six weeks. If you have longer hair and you intend on letting your hair grow even longer, the cut can be done every six months. You also want to check your hair regularly; if you have split ends or your hair's overall health looks dull, you'd need to get it trimmed. Trimming doesn't take too much off the length. It can just be an inch or two off the ends to maintain your hair's health.

**Bleaching Your Own Hair**

In a single word: Don't! Do not, under any circumstances, try to bleach your own hair at home. There is a reason why salons exist and why people have dedicated the better part of their lives to studying how to dye, cut and style hair. Always leave it to the professionals. You will not get salon-quality results unless you go to a salon. Store-bought hair bleach is not as strong as salon bleach. If you have longer hair, you may end up with patchy results or hair that has been underdeveloped. Knowing the role temperature plays in developing the bleach in your hair is also essential. Your hair is a unique tone, thickness, and quality. There are so many variables to work with. Chances are you will visit a salon afterward to fix the damage, which can prove a bit embarrassing. You might have to consider cutting it shorter if it was once long. Trust me on this one!

**General Body and Hygiene Care**

Taking care of your hygiene is essential not only for you and your overall health but also for your interactions with other people. You probably know everything there is to know about keeping your body clean and healthy, but let us take a quick recap.

### DENTAL HYGIENE

If you can't see a dentist at least once a year, every second year should be fine, provided you take care of your teeth daily. Brushing your teeth daily with fluoride toothpaste and gargling with mouthwash is important.

| BRUSH TEETH REGULARLY | USE A FLUORIDE TOOTHPASTE | FLOSS ONCE A DAY | SEE A DENTIST REGULARLY |
|---|---|---|---|
| DO NOT SMOKE | CONSIDER A MOUTHWASH | LIMIT SUGARY FOODS, STARCHES | DRINK MORE WATER |

Brush your teeth every morning and before you go to bed as a minimum. If you can also brush after every meal, that is better. Flossing is imperative for having healthy teeth and gums. Avoid eating sugary sweets and soft drinks, as this can cause damage to your teeth over time. Smoking is something that also causes damage to your teeth by causing discoloration. It also causes gum disease and slows healing for any mouth sores or injuries that you may get. Having a healthy white smile and fresh breath are attractive features. These features can naturally make you feel more socially confident.

## BODY HYGIENE

We know how important it is to shower or bathe every day. Whether it is winter or summer, we sweat. Bathing and showering make sure that we don't develop any odors. Showering also benefits our bodies by improving circulation, removing toxins, and reducing stress. It also enhances our lung function and allows us to sleep better.

Once clean, you can also reduce the reoccurrence of body odor by using sprays, perfumes, and deodorants.

Your daily showers don't need to be more than five to ten minutes. How often you shower is significantly impacted by the type of work you do daily. Chances are, if you sit in an office at a desk all day, you may not need a second shower when you get home. Still, you may need one if you work as a janitor, fishmonger, refuse removal, or return from a workout.

It is also essential to always keep your genital area clean. Ladies, use sanitary towels and wipes to keep yourself feeling clean and fresh, especially during menstruation. Remember that you can't flush these items down the toilet. Specialized cleansers are also available designed for these areas. Standard shower gels can be too perfumed and irritate. If this is the case, these cleansers are readily available in stores.

## SHAVING

As a woman, you may or may not want to shave, which is entirely up to you. As a man, you may want to shave or grow your beard. Whatever choices you make and if you decide to shave, this should be done properly. If not done correctly, you may experience ingrown hairs or discomfort.

If you are shaving your face, you will start by placing a wet cloth on your face that has been soaked in warm water. Do this for a few minutes before rubbing the shaving cream generously onto your face. Then begin shaving in the direction that your hair grows. This will give you the best results.

## PHYSICAL FITNESS AND HEALTH

Staying active is an integral part of maintaining your overall health. It poses a lot of benefits, and even if you feel like you have absolutely no time to go to the gym, working out at home does your body a lot of good. You will save money by visiting the doctor less, dramatically reducing your risks of depression and anxiety. You will have an improved quality of life because you won't have aches and pains every time you stand up and move around. You will be less prone to injury and increase your overall life expectancy (Mana Medical Associates, 2017).

Walking, jogging, riding a bicycle, swimming, and other sports you may enjoy are great ways to stay fit. You could even take your dog for a walk, providing you with more health benefits than you'd get if you were sitting on the couch at home. Strength training and getting your muscles moving and active is an excellent way of ensuring you don't lose any muscle strength. Doing tai chi and playing sports are also great for keeping your body in good shape (Harvard Health Publishing, 2019).

The thing about doing exercise is getting into a daily exercise routine. This means making time for a workout until it becomes a natural part of your day. This doesn't need to take up more than ten minutes a day. It is a well-known fact that if you don't use it, you will lose it. This doesn't mean that your bicep will fall out of your arm, but rather it means that you will lose strength in your muscles if you don't use them. Here are five quick exercises that you can do during your day to keep your body strong (Davis, 2020):

## Lunges

Putting one foot forward, go down to your knee in a controlled motion.

## Push-ups

Laying flat on the floor on your stomach, push up from the ground with your arms while keeping your back straight.

## Squats

Keeping your feet shoulder length apart and your back straight, bend your knees and go down to the ground as low as you can.

## Dumbbell Presses

You can lift your weights straight above your head with your arms going upwards at the side of your head. If you don't have dumbbells, grab some canned foods or water bottles from the kitchen and get creative.

**Burpees**

One of the best ways to get the heart rate pumping and the blood flowing is to do burpees. It also increases your strength dramatically.

**Staying Healthy**

Being fat doesn't always mean you're unhealthy, and being thin doesn't always mean you're healthy. Health is determined by what you eat, what you put into your body, and ensuring that you treat your body well. This means maintaining a healthy BMI, eating nutritious foods, and avoiding junk foods. Suppose you struggle to follow a healthy lifestyle or don't know what to eat. In that case, it is always best to speak to a doctor or a dietician to ensure you are within a healthy BMI range.

It's also easy to fall into unhealthy eating habits when facing emotional challenges. One way of overcoming this is by ensuring that your home is stocked with healthy and nutritious snacks rather than unhealthy foods.

## HEALTHY SLEEPING

Sleep is an essential part of our lives. We spend a third of our lives sleeping. If you want a healthy life, you must ensure that your sleep health and your sleeping routines are up to scratch. Many people often neglect sleep. There are so many other things we would rather be doing than laying in bed for eight hours doing absolutely nothing. But when you are sleeping, you are not doing "nothing." Your body is recuperating, it is healing itself, and it is getting itself back to optimal functionality.

Everyday things standing in the way of us getting a good night's sleep can include; a busy lifestyle, a change in your biological clock caused by hormonal changes, starting your day too early in the morning, gaming, watching TV, doing homework, studying or working late into the night.

Not getting enough sleep can cause mental impairments, affecting your work at school, college, or your job. It can also lead to you being moodier, experiencing erratic behavior, and not being able to do your best at sports.

The best way to create healthy sleeping habits is by finding and sticking to a daily routine. Turn off all electronics an hour before you intend to sleep, including your phone. Give yourself some quiet time which will make it easier to fall asleep. Once you have your sleep schedule and a good routine, you must stick to it, even on weekends. It's also essential to ensure that your room is dark and quiet when you are sleeping and that your bed is only kept for sleeping. This means keeping food, laptops, and notebooks off the bed. Keeping your bedroom clean, clutter-free, and not too warm or cold will also help.

DRESS TO IMPRESS

The first impression you usually make on strangers is based on your clothes and how you dress well before you open your mouth. Moreover, how you see yourself is greatly influenced by what you wear and how you feel about what you wear.

When you wear clothes, it is essential to know your measurements and to buy clothes that fit you. Don't buy clothes with the hopes of losing weight and fitting into them. That will make you feel uncomfortable in the brand-new clothes you should enjoy wearing.

It is also important to wear the right clothes for the right occasion.

**Interview**

Dressing for an interview is a great time to keep it simple yet extremely neat. In the past, you needed to maintain a very rigid standard of attire when going for an interview. This was a full suit and tie for men and a formal dress and heels for women. This standard has become a lot more relaxed nowadays. It is still crucial to ensure that you are dressed appropriately in neatly ironed clothes. Keeping a shirt and tie for men and a formal dress or suit for women will still do extremely well for the purpose. Tip: If you are in contact with the recruiter, it's worth asking what their interview dress code expectations are. Note that a trendy marketing or design company might look for a little flare or personality so you stand out from the rest but keep it subtle to be safe. Make sure you don't go over-the-top on the jewelry or makeup and aren't wearing excessively revealing clothes. Then let your skills speak for themselves.

PURCHASING CLOTHES

When shopping for clothes, remember to always choose quality over quantity. You want to make sure that you purchase clothes that will last longer, are made from quality materials, and feel good on your skin. Higher quality items will also give you a better fit. You also won't be throwing clothing items out as often, which is excellent news for the environment.

It is also important to know where your clothing was made to ensure you buy fair trade items.

When you are buying clothes, it is best to avoid online shopping. Sizes usually aren't what you'd get in-store, and you may find yourself with a horrible knock-off of what you saw on the site.

You don't actually need a lot of clothes. Instead, you need a few good items that can be matched with each other. This will give you a variation of outfits without breaking the bank and buying a new wardrobe every month. Also, don't worry about repeating an outfit. No one wears a new outfit every day except for celebrities. If you have quality clothing items and can wash and clean them, that is reason enough for you to wear the same outfit more than once.

Lastly, don't allow a store to dictate how you feel about your body. Many stores only stock items for one body type. This means that you may not find your perfect fit or may feel uncomfortable in the purchased clothes.

Remember that this is not a reflection of your appearance but the target market the store hopes to appeal to. You are beautiful and unique! Your clothing and size do not determine your worth!

# HEALTH INSURANCE AND FIRST AID KNOW-HOWS

The last thing you want is to get sick or injured in a new town or country and not know where the nearest hospital or doctor is. While some injuries and illnesses need medical attention, others can be treated at home as long as you have the right supplies.

## FILLING IN FORMS

Whether you are headed to the emergency room or signing documentation for your new medical insurance, you will need to know how to fill out a form. This is one of the most simple things to do, but it may appear harder than it is. Firstly, you must ensure that you never sign something you disagree with or don't understand. When you are asked to initial each page of a contract, it shows that you have read and understood everything on that page. Your signature or initials are proof of that.

Filling out information on a form would require you to know things like your identity or passport number, your social security number in the US or your national insurance or NHS number in the UK, your address, your contact details, your date of birth, and a variety of other information. Medical-related forms may ask for your medical history and if you are allergic to any medications.

When you sign a contract or a document, you will need to fill in the location where you signed the document, the date, and sometimes the time. You will include your signature and your name in full as it appears on your official identity document. It's handy to have the contact details of someone close to you. They can serve as an emergency contact, a next of kin, or an alternate contact person if you can't be reached for any reason.

## MEDICAL INSURANCE

Whether you are in an area or country that offers comprehensive medical cover like the UK or whether you are in a country that offers no free health cover.

Private medical insurance is always worth considering. In some states within the US, medical insurance is not only recommended but also required. Unfortunately, health care is not always readily and freely available to people. The alternative to not having medical or health insurance is usually exorbitant fees that may lead to bankruptcy, especially in accidents or severe illnesses. But no one should be punished for being sick or having an accident.

Here are some things you should know about health insurance in the US:

• You have cover for young adult coverage on your parent's health insurance until you are 26 years of age. You qualify for this adult coverage whether or not you live with your parents, are financially dependent on them, have kids of your own, are married, or are eligible to get your own coverage (Assistant Secretary for Public Affairs) ASPA), 2013).

• You may be eligible for public programs such as Medicaid or the Children's Health Insurance Program (CHIP), which is available for children under the age of 19 (KidsHealth, 2018).

• You will need to sign up for healthcare plans during the open enrollment period. This is a time of the year when you can sign up or enroll for medical insurance, or you can change the current plan you are on. This works for health insurance provided by your place of work, Medicare, or through the Affordable Care Act (ACA) (UHS, n.d.).

- In the US, free healthcare is not readily available, and you need to have medical insurance to be treated.

- In the US, you can also access healthcare through your employer. They may pay a contribution of up to 75% of your health insurance premiums, which is standard practice when working in the US. In other countries with free healthcare, employers may offer healthcare insurance. Still, it is often seen as something nice to have in your back pocket rather than a necessity.

In the UK, as a resident, you are entitled to free healthcare treatment through the National Health Service (NHS). This service provides you with medical treatment that covers a wide array of illnesses and accidents. However, suppose you hope to have access to private services such as; a more comprehensive array of medications, quicker treatment, and the luxury of sleeping in a private room during your hospital stay. You may consider signing up for private medical insurance if that's the case.

While it may be a bit expensive to consider private medical insurance at a young age in the UK. It is worth considering as you age and as ailments naturally become more prevalent. The best way to get private medical insurance is by signing up with a broker, an insurance advisor, or anywhere else that offers the service of signing you up.

When signing up for medical insurance, it is always important to read your policies very closely and question anything you may not understand.

Suppose you hope to get private healthcare insurance and are not covered by your employer or your parent's family plan. In that case, you can check government sites to see what free plans you may qualify for, and you can use these sources to compare different plans before choosing the one that best suits you.

DENTAL INSURANCE

Dental care is sometimes covered in your insurance plan. Still, check how much of the payment is covered, what treatments are covered, and at which facilities. If dental care is not covered in your health insurance plan, it may be available as its own plan. In the UK, you can access free dental care up to 18 or 19 years of age if you are enrolled in full-time education.

You can receive dental care from dental schools or dental clinics, community clinics, and clinical trials in the US.

The best insurance is to look after your teeth and avoid needing emergency dental care.

When and Where to Seek Medical Help

When you move to a new area, the first thing you are going to want to do is to familiarize yourself with the lay of the land. Find the nearest clinic, doctor, and hospital, find out where the vet is if you have a pet, and find the quickest routes to these places.

Sometimes, it is difficult to know that you are in the middle of an emergency, especially when you live alone. You may underestimate your symptoms, and this may delay you in seeking medical care.

If you feel dysfunctional and can't go about your day without feeling tired, it may warrant a visit to the doctor. Suppose you have an extensive fever, can barely keep your eyes open, and struggle to carry out necessary tasks. In that case, you may need to get to the hospital. If you find yourself severely injured and feel like you may pass out, call for help as soon as possible. Be sure to leave a door unlatched so those who are there to help you can quickly get into your home.

## EMERGENCY CONTACTS

The first thing you will do when you move into your new home is—make a list of all emergency numbers and have them placed somewhere where you can quickly see them. You don't want it hidden in a drawer where you must rummage through piles of paper to locate it. Have it displayed on the fridge or your coffee table, making it easily accessible.

**IN THE UK, YOU CAN CALL 111 FOR MEDICAL ADVICE AND 999 FOR MEDICAL EMERGENCIES. IN THE US, YOU WILL CALL 911 IN CASE OF AN EMERGENCY.**

Depending on where you stay, emergency numbers for different services may vary.

## FIRST AID

The reality is that cuts and scrapes, burns, and bruises happen. But a basic understanding of first aid can help you when you're alone and keep you in one piece until you make your way to the emergency room or an urgent care clinic.

## Cuts and Wounds

If a wound is bleeding quite a bit, you will ensure that nothing is stuck in the wounded area. You will put pressure on the wound with a cloth for ten minutes. You will ensure that you raise the injury so that it is above the level of your heart to reduce blood flow. If the wound does not stop bleeding, replace the cloth with a new and clean one and continue applying pressure. If possible, you may want to tie a belt or something similar above the wound to help with reducing bleeding.

Once the bleeding has stopped, you will need to clean around the wound with soap or an antiseptic wash, making sure not to get anything directly into the wound. Pat, dry the area with sterile gauze and wrap it with a sterile bandage. You are going to do this to minimize infection as much as possible.

**FIRST AID FOR CUTS**

WASH THE WOUND | SQUEEZE THE EDGES OF THE WOUND | DISINFECT THE EDGES OF THE WOUND | APPLY A CLEAN BANDAGE | IF MUSCLES OR TENDONS ARE INJURED, CALL A DOCTOR

Suppose the wound does get infected and has pus that is changing color. In that case, you will need to seek medical attention as soon as possible to take antibiotics and clean the infected area. You can manage your pain with over-the-counter pain management medication.

**Burns**

If you experience a burn, you will want to remove the heat from the burn (take your hand off the stove, although I'm sure this happened automatically).

**FIRST AID TIPS FOR BURNS**

| RINSE WITH COLD WATER | PUT ON A STERILE BANDAGE | PLENTIFUL DRINK | TAKE PAINKILLERS | DOCTOR'S CALL |

**NOT TO BE DONE ON BURNS**

| DO NOT USE OIL | DO NOT WIPE THE WOUND WITH ALCOHOL | DO NOT APPLY ICE DIRECTLY TO THE BURN | CAN'T POP BUBBLES | DO NOT TEAR OFF THE STUCK CLOTHES |

You will make sure to remove anything around the burn, like clothes or jewelry, but do not remove anything that may be burnt onto the skin. You will run the affected area under cool water for around 20 minutes. Be sure not to put ice on the wound, and do not use home remedies like butter or toothpaste. You can also take over-the-counter medications to reduce any pain.

You will need to seek medical attention if the burn is severe, caused by chemicals, or if you may have inhaled any smoke.

**Colds and Flus**

You may have a cold or flu if you feel under the weather. Your body will be working hard to fight off whatever is infecting your body, which may cause a fever and other related symptoms. You will have either a viral or bacterial infection. Antibiotics won't work on viruses.

You can best treat your symptoms by taking over-the-counter medications for pain, headaches, and fevers. Having cough syrup if you have a cough or a tight chest. Using nasal spray and cold and flu medication for a blocked and runny nose. You will also need to stay home, rest, hydrate, and eat well. If you find that you're not getting better after three to four days or your symptoms are worsening, you will want to head to the doctor for stronger medication.

## First Aid Kit

First aid is not just about having a box with medical supplies. It also means knowing how to; help someone choking by performing the Heimlich maneuver (fists at the stomach where the ribs meet, putting pressure, and thrusting upwards). As well as knowing the basics of CPR (pumping to the beat of Staying Alive by the Bee Gees).

The best thing you can do when you are moving out on your own is to take a CPR or first aid class and be sure to get all the supplies you may need for a first aid kit. This is what you should have in your first aid kit (NHS Choices, 2019):

- different size band-aids
- gauze and dressing
- bandages
- safety pins
- sterile gloves
- tweezers
- scissors
- sterile cleansing wipes
- a thermometer
- an antihistamine
- over-the-counter pain medications
- distilled water

- eye wash station

Today most of the above can be bought in an already-put-together kit. But it is good for you to know what should be in it, what instance you may need its contents and how to use them.

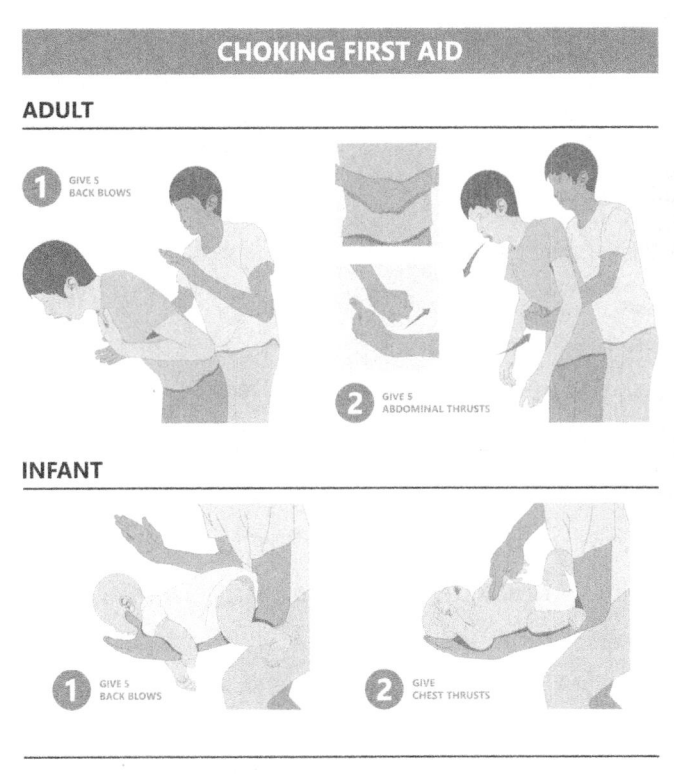

### CHOKING FIRST AID

**ADULT**

1. GIVE 5 BACK BLOWS
2. GIVE 5 ABDOMINAL THRUSTS

**INFANT**

1. GIVE 5 BACK BLOWS
2. GIVE CHEST THRUSTS

REPEAT STEP 1 AND 2 UNTIL THE OBJECT UNTIL THE OBJECT IS EJECTED OR THE PERSON FORCEFULLY COUGHS

DIAL FOR AN AMBULANCE IMMEDIATELY IF THE OBJECT HAS NOT DISLODGED AFTER 3 REPETITIONS OF STEP 1 AND 2

# FORMING SAFE AND HEALTHY RELATIONSHIPS

*H*umans are social beings. Whether we are introverted or extroverted, we thrive off companionship. We need other people to survive. That is just the way the human mind works. Therefore, forming healthy, safe relationships with everyone around us is essential. Trust must be the foundation of every good relationship, whether spending time with family, making new friends, or dating.

## ROMANTIC RELATIONSHIPS

Each person is different and what they look for in a relationship is different. Whatever you may be looking for, it is essential to find someone with whom you are completely comfortable. Be with someone who accepts you for who you are. It can get exhausting if you have to pretend to be someone you are not or if you have to change things about yourself when you are with a person. Be with someone that allows you to be the most authentic version of yourself.

When you find someone you like and start dating, it is important not to forget about your friends. Yes, you may have less time for outings with your friends as you accommodate a new person in your life that you are spending time. Still, each person in our lives pours something different into our beings. Having friends as support is extremely important, so make sure not to cut your friends out entirely when you start dating someone.

Remember, when you date someone, you are still your own person. There will be things they love doing that you don't enjoy much and vice versa. This is perfectly fine and normal, and it is actually a good thing. Take the time to do the things you both enjoy separately. This will allow you to continuously remember who you are.

Every relationship will face challenges. Communicating and addressing the challenges is essential so that it doesn't fester into something bigger than it initially was. As unique individuals, you and your partner will have differing views and opinions on certain things. This is normal and healthy. Conflict will arise, and it is actually healthy to argue. But it is also essential to know the difference between positive conflict, which helps you grow as a couple, and negative conflict, which targets you as a person and victimizes you.

A good relationship has mutual respect. A good relationship is one where your partner asks for your opinion and respects it even if it differs from theirs. A good relationship is based on trust and honesty. These three pillars form the foundation for a strong relationship.

When you engage in a relationship, it is essential to notice any signs that may lead you to believe the relationship is abusive or toxic. Listen to those around you. Love is blind, but those closest to you may see some red flags before you do. Listen to them and try to attune yourself to the things happening around you that they see and that you may miss. Abuse isn't always physical or verbal. Abuse can be emotional, making you feel bad about yourself and cutting you off from those around you. It may make you feel like you are being controlled and forced to turn into a different person they like better. These forms of abuse are usually more subtle and may even be harder to notice. But red flags are always around.

If you are in an unhealthy relationship, the power lies with you to end the relationship. Sometimes, you need to step back and ask yourself if your friend was in the same relationship you are in and if they were being treated the way you are. Would you respect that and be happy with it? Or would you do whatever it takes to help them get out of that relationship?

Suppose you feel like you can't leave the relationship or escape. In that case, there are places that you can reach out to for support and help in leaving an abusive relationship. Suppose you are in danger or feel like you are in immediate danger. In that case, you should contact emergency services, and they will dispatch a police officer to you. If you cannot talk on the phone, dispatch agents will guide you to speak as if you were ordering a pizza or speaking to a delivery person.

## SEX AND RELATIONSHIPS

Just dating someone does not mean you should be having sex. Sex does not define a relationship, and it does not make a relationship real. Relationships are made up of so many other important aspects. Still, society has distorted the concept of relationships into being entirely about sex. The second you feel pressurized by your partner or anyone else outside of your relationship to have sex, you should back away. Set clear boundaries, and make it clear that you will engage in acts of intimacy when you are ready.

You need to wait until you are ready. It is also perfectly acceptable to change your mind about being ready. You are not leading anyone on by saying you are not ready, even if you thought you were. Intimacy is a big deal, and it should not be downplayed. A partner that respects you will respect your decision about sex, and they won't force you into anything you are uncomfortable with.

## ONLINE DATING

Safety is the most important aspect if you decide to pursue online dating. Always be careful of the information you share with someone, no matter how much you like the person you are chatting with.

SWIPE RIGHT

Don't give out information about your family or your personal and banking information. If you do decide to meet the person face to face, make sure it is in a crowded place and that someone you trust knows where you are at all times. If you feel uncomfortable at any point, do not be afraid to leave. You can even communicate with bartenders or wait staff to help you if you are feeling unsafe.

## MAKING FRIENDS

It may feel like the older you get, the harder it is to make friends. It seems like young kids effortlessly walk into friendships, but this is not always the case when you get older. Don't be afraid to take the initiative. You may find yourself immediately drawn to some people and their personalities. In such cases, invite them for coffee or for lunch. Some friendships may immediately blossom, and others may fizzle out, which is alright. Find the people that you are most comfortable with, as you should in every other relationship. Tip: Be yourself, and let people see the real you; otherwise, you may come across as guarded and ingenuine. Be genuine, and you are more likely to attract real friends with similar personalities and likes, friends that will make you feel happy to be you.

## KNOWING YOUR WORTH AND BEING POSITIVE

Our emotions control the way we view and perceive the world. You know how you can't seem to go somewhere because it reminds you of something sad? This aspect of your physical world is tainted by the pain caused by an emotion. Emotions have the power to ruin our days or to make our days the most joyful and fulfilling they have ever been. But it's important to remember that you control your emotions. Your emotions don't control you. Having a better grasp of your feelings will change how you perceive the world and allow you to be a more positive person.

## EMOTIONAL INTELLIGENCE

Your emotional intelligence allows you to perceive, control, and evaluate emotions. It is a topic of much debate, with some saying that you can grow your emotional intelligence and others saying that you are born with it (Cherry, 2022).

Having high emotional intelligence means that you can perceive the emotions of others and respond appropriately to what they may be exhibiting. It means that you can control your own emotions. You don't have erratic emotional outbursts at every turn; you can evaluate emotions and assess your emotional responses to certain situations.

Emotional intelligence is crucial because it allows you to accept criticism without feeling victimized or taking it personally. It helps you understand and move past a mistake you may have made without dwelling on it or living with self-pity. It allows you to safely agree and disagree when needed, and it will enable you to share your feelings with others and understand the feelings of others while working toward a beneficial solution for all parties involved.

Emotional intelligence also allows you to empathize with others and metaphorically put yourself in their shoes. It enables you to have excellent listening skills, hearing what people have to say and what lies heavy on their hearts. It also helps you understand why you and others may respond to certain situations in a specific way. It allows you to reflect on your response and reactions and tally whether your reactions were rational or irrational.

## DEALING WITH EMOTIONS

We can't shove our emotions down, we can't bury them, we can't hide them, and we can't pretend like they don't exist. The only way to deal with our emotions is to acknowledge them and understand why we feel strongly about something.

When experiencing a big emotion, whether it makes us feel good or bad, you need to experience it fully. Sit with the feeling, ask yourself why it is arising and ask yourself what you can do to feel this way again or to avoid feeling this way.

It is also essential to never make big decisions when experiencing big emotions. Don't post your emotions on social media, and don't act on these feelings too quickly without considering the rationality behind these feelings (Miller, 2021).

## KNOW YOUR MANNERS

Manners are an important social construct that follows us from childhood into adulthood. As you get older, your manners will change.

You will need to make sure you have what is considered good manners. Such as; apologizing for doing something wrong, asking for permission to do things, or gaining consent to touch something that doesn't belong to you. Knowing the importance of face-to-face interactions, learning not to answer a phone call or respond to a text or message when speaking to someone face-to-face or on a dinner date. Not talking over someone when they are speaking. You will also need to know that making eye contact is extremely important (Witmer, 2019).

## ETIQUETTE

Certain types of etiquette need to be adhered to in social interactions. For example, if you bump into someone while walking, you will apologize to them before walking on. If you are invited to a birthday party, you will be sure to show up with a gift in hand. And if you are at a fancy restaurant, you would be sure to use a knife and fork when eating instead of your hands.

## FORMAL TABLE SETTING

- Bread Plate
- Butter Knife
- Dessert Spoon
- Dessert Fork
- Red wine glass
- Water glass
- White wine glass
- Salad Fork
- Fish Fork
- Dinner Fork
- Serving Plate
- Dinner knife
- Fish Knife
- Salad Knife
- Soup Spoon

If you are hosting an event or a party, there is some etiquette that you would adhere to. You will need to plan well in advance and ensure that all your guests know they are invited. You will need to be welcoming and accommodating. As the common factor among all your guests, you must be entertaining.

If you are invited as a guest, always RSVP on time. If you are attending, be sure to be on time. The host may refuse, but always offer to help, even if you aren't actually going to help. Lastly, thank your host for the invite and the awesome party.

## STAYING POSITIVE

When you are positive about the world, you attract positivity too. Being someone who can find joy in the simple things is one way of ensuring that you always face the world with a positive outlook.

When you have a positive outlook on life, you are more likely to have a more robust and better immune system. You will feel stronger physically, and the negativity will become harder to notice.

## LOVING-KINDNESS MEDITATION

Meditation is an excellent way of getting in touch with a more positive part of yourself. For far too long, meditation has been seen as a spiritual practice. And while it is a highly spiritual act, anyone can use it to be more grateful, kind, and loving. The thing is, you can't be loving toward others until you start showing love toward yourself and until you are kind to yourself. Loving-kindness meditation is where you spend a few minutes each day in the quiet, breathing deeply and thinking positive thoughts about yourself and about others. It doesn't have to be a long meditation time, but starting your day off with this positivity for five minutes will make a notable difference in your life.

## LOVE yourself

### THINK OF THE BEST VERSION OF YOURSELF

Think about where you are now and what goals you have for yourself. Once they have all been achieved, the goals you envision for yourself will probably allow you to be the best version of yourself. Being positive goes far beyond the here and now and beyond present mindfulness. It has been proven that if you think positively about a future version of yourself, this version has accomplished everything the current you are hoping to achieve, and you will feel more positive (The Syndicate Post, 2016).

### GET RID OF NEGATIVITY

This is going to take some conscious effort. Still, you must make sure you purposefully relinquish the negative thoughts you may find yourself thinking. When presented with a scenario that is easy to take as a negative occurrence, look at the positive side. For example, if you have spilled coffee on your shirt before leaving home, think of it as an opportunity to wear the new shirt that has been in your closet for weeks.

Make a conscious effort to search for positivity in a situation. Always look on the bright side of life. (Graham Chapman, Life of Brian)

REMOVE TOXIC FRIENDS

If you have people in your life constantly pushing you down, always pointing out your flaws, and never having anything good to say, they are not your people. Find people with positive things to say, are kind, bring out the best in you, and lift you up instead of pushing you down. The people you surround yourself with are a mirror reflection of who you are. For you to be positive, you need to surround yourself with people who are positive too.

CELEBRATE YOUR ACCOMPLISHMENTS

It isn't bragging; you have every reason to be proud of yourself and proud of your accomplishments. You can do amazing things, and you should celebrate the things you have already achieved. This could be for tests you've passed, the money you raised for charity, sporting events, or getting your first part-time job.

## ASKING FOR HELP

Whether it is a physical load that you are carrying or an emotional one, asking for help is something that no one should ever shy away from. There has been a negative notion around the idea of asking for help. Everyone thinks that asking for help is for the weak, but this is quite the contrary. Asking for help means you are solid and secure enough to seek the help you need. Whether you ask someone to help you carry your groceries up the stairs or life seems way too overwhelming. If you need to ask someone for emotional and mental support, don't be afraid to do so.

People often avoid asking for help because they are scared. They are afraid of what others may say or do, or they are embarrassed, and sometimes they may not even know what to say when they ask for help. But anyone who cares about you would love to help you.

There are many people that you can ask for help. You can ask for help from anyone you trust and are comfortable with, whether a friend, parent, sibling, or professional. The important thing is knowing and understanding that you deserve support. It may take courage, but asking for help will always be positive.

## KNOW YOUR SELF-WORTH

The world consists of give-and-take. What you put out to the world will be reciprocated back to you. The same goes for your own self-worth and how you value yourself. How you see yourself is how the world will see you and how the world will treat you. This is very apparent in physical relationships. If you value and respect your body, others will see and show respect. The opposite occurs if you don't respect or love yourself.

If you lack confidence and question your every move, this energy will be seen, and the world will take advantage of you. But if you see yourself as strong and confident, this is what the world will see and how the world will treat you.

Knowing your self-worth is essential for self-awareness and understanding who you are. Taking up the space in the world you deserve. It helps you boost your self-esteem, especially when you realize just how unique you are.

**Recognizing Your Self-Worth**

This is something that many people struggle with—they don't often realize their self-worth. Whether they try to be humble or fit in, it is never a good thing to dim your shine for any reason. There are some steps you can follow to recognize your self-worth (OutOfStress, 2021):

- Know yourself—knowing yourself is essential to knowing your self-worth. You will know what you are best at and how to always put your best foot forward. This can be hard, just like a self-evaluation is really hard. You may be worried about over or under-valuing yourself. To become self-aware, you need to ask yourself a few questions. What makes you happy? What makes you sad? What are you good at? What are your greatest strengths? What are your greatest weaknesses? How can you improve yourself?
- Forgive yourself—the easiest person to hold a grudge against you is yourself. It is easy to hold on to what you have done wrong in the past, and it is easy to forget the things that you have done right. Forgiving yourself is the next step you can take to learn your value.
- Have personal time—Make time for yourself and learn who you are. You are constantly adapting and changing as a human, so having personal time is a must.
- Increase your self-love—fall in love with the little things you do, fall in love with your quirks, whether they are small or defining

factors in your life, and you will see the world falling in love with these parts of you too.
- Say no—some things take away from you more than they give to you. Learn to say no to those things and those people.
- Be with like-minded people—be with people who are also surrounding themselves with positivity, who are also finding their self-worth, and who want to make the world happier.
- You will then be able to better recognize your self-worth and show the world who you really are.

Knowing your self-worth allows you to assert yourself and be the best version of yourself. You can set clear and achievable goals, speak up for yourself, and form healthier relationships. Over and above that, you will have a greater sense of self-love, and you will enjoy spending time alone with yourself. You will meet a new, confident version of yourself (OutOfStress, 2021).

# AFTERWORD

Being an adult is certainly not easy. There are so many things you need to keep track of and stay on top of that it is easy to become overwhelmed. The worst part is that we are often ill-prepared as youngsters for all this responsibility we will need to take on.

While your responsibilities won't be lessened, this book has been written in the hopes that it will help you better prepare for a life that is to come. A life that is; fulfilling and happy. And preparedness enables you to always stay on top of things.

As you venture into the seemingly never-ending journey of adulthood, all you need to know is that life is as fulfilling as you allow it to be. By combining everything I have mentioned in this book, you will find happiness and positivity even in the small and mundane things in life. Do you have to spend the weekend cleaning your home? No problem! The positive side is that you can listen to your favorite playlist or watch your favorite Netflix series. You will quickly realize how you feel reflected by how your home is kept. Once you get into the routine of staying on top of your chores and tasks, it will come naturally to you. You will feel happy and fulfilled, and you will find pride in every task you have fulfilled.

So let us embark on this journey into adulthood. I am so happy to be joining you. You got this!

If you enjoyed the book, please leave a review. It makes all the difference and helps others find and learn about this resource.

Thanks so much, Katie x

ALSO BY KATIE WEBSDELL

Adult Life Skills for Older Teens: Money & Work Edition (Vol. 2)

Adult Life Skills for Older Teens: THE BIG ONE (Vol. 1 & 2)

# BIBLIOGRAPHY

Ariel. (n.d.). *Washing Symbols and Labels on Clothes Explained.* Www.ariel.co.uk. https://www.ariel.co.uk/en-gb/how-to-wash/how-to-do-laundry/fabric-care-labels

Aspire. (2020, July 28). *How To Stop Or Fix A Squeaky Door and Best Lubricant For Door Hinges.* Aspire Doors. https://www.aspiredoors.co.uk/blog/how-to-stop-a-squeaky-door

Assistant Secretary for Public Affairs (ASPA). (2013, March 12). *Young Adult Coverage.* HHS.gov. https://www.hhs.gov/healthcare/about-the-aca/young-adult-coverage/index.html

Atomic Dermatology. (2018, November 12). *Skin Care: Why It's Important to Take Care of Your Skin.* Atomic Dermatology. https://www.atomicderm.com/skin-care-why-its-important-to-take-care-of-your-skin/

Becker, J. (2022, March 28). *What Bills to Expect When Renting an Apartment? | CLFA.* Cass Lake Front Apartments. https://clfapartments.com/what-bills-to-expect-when-renting-an-apartment/

Berry, J. (2019, March 14). *The 8 best practices for healthy teeth and gums.* Www.medicalnewstoday.com. https://www.medicalnewstoday.com/articles/324708#not-smoking

Bissegger, T. (n.d.). *14 basic cooking terms everyone should know.* Hospitalityinsights.ehl.edu. https://hospitalityinsights.ehl.edu/cooking-terms

Bright Network. (n.d.). *What to wear to an interview.* Bright Network. https://www.brightnetwork.co.uk/graduate-career-advice/telephone-video-interviews/what-to-wear/

Callahan, T. P. (2020, October 28). *15 Tips To Get Your FULL Security Deposit Back From Your Landlord.* Moversville. https://moversville.com/blog/get-security-deposit-back

Campion, A. (2022). *Home maintenance checklist.* Www.confused.com.

https://www.confused.com/home-insurance/guides/monthly-maintenance-checks-for-your-home

Chen, J. (2022). *Security Deposit*. Investopedia. https://www.investopedia.com/terms/s/security-deposit.asp

Cherry, K. (2022, August 3). Overview of emotional intelligence. Verywell Mind. https://www.verywellmind.com/what-is-emotional-intelligence-2795423

CHOC Children. (n.d.). *Sleep Hygiene for Teens*. https://www.choc.org/wp/wp-content/uploads/2016/04/Sleep-Hygiene-Teen-Handout.pdf

Citizens Advice. (n.d.). *Getting your tenancy deposit back*. Www.citizensadvice.org.uk. https://www.citizensadvice.org.uk/housing/renting-privately/ending-your-tenancy/getting-your-tenancy-deposit-back/

Clarke, E. (2019, September 5). *Baked Salmon in Foil | Easy, Healthy Recipe*. Well Plated by Erin. https://www.wellplated.com/baked-salmon-in-foil/

Cohen, J. (2022). *5 Exercises That Burn a Ton of Calories*. Health. https://www.health.com/fitness/5-exercises-that-burn-the-most-calories

Collins, L. (2022, February 14). *6 Reasons Why You Shouldn't Bleach Your Hair Yourself*. LKC Studios - Have a Good Hair Day. https://laurakcollins.com/6-reasons-why-you-shouldnt-bleach-hair-at-home/

David Lowery Quotes. (n.d.). *BrainyQuote*. https://www.brainyquote.com/citation/quotes/david_lowery_896832

Davis, N. (2020, September 24). *10 Best Exercises for Everyone*. Healthline. https://www.healthline.com/health/fitness-exercise/10-best-exercises-everyday#start-here

DiBiase, D. (2021). *How to feel better: Tips for self-care when sick | What's Up at Upstate | SUNY Upstate Medical University*. Www.upstate.edu. https://www.upstate.edu/whatsup/2020/0515-how-to-feel-better-tips-for-self-care-when-sick.php

Dove, H., & Mchale, E. (2020). *Best vegetables to grow on your windowsill | Kew*. Www.kew.org. https://www.kew.org/read-and-watch/windowsill-veg-herbs

## BIBLIOGRAPHY | 173

Edwards, M. (n.d.). *How to Clean and Maintain Guttering Systems.* DIY Doctor. https://www.diydoctor.org.uk/projects/cleaning-gutters.htm

Elkins, K. (2017, December 27). *6 basic knife skills you should master in your 20s.* CNBC. https://www.cnbc.com/2017/12/27/6-basic-knife-skills-you-should-master-in-your-20s.html

Emily Post. (n.d.). *Party Etiquette Tips for Hosts and Guests.* Emily Post. https://emilypost.com/advice/party-etiquette-tips-for-hosts-and-guests

Eschner, K. (2017). *Why the Can Opener Wasn't Invented Until Almost 50 Years After the Can.* Smithsonian Magazine. https://www.smithsonianmag.com/smart-news/why-can-opener-wasnt-invented-until-almost-50-years-after-can-180964590/#:~:text=The%20first%20-can%20opener%20was%20actually%20an%20American%20invention%2C%20patented

Fleur & Bee. (2020). *The Best Skin Care Routine for Your 20s.* Fleur & Bee. https://fleurandbee.com/blogs/news/best-skin-care-routine-for-20s

Floyd, A. (2020, May 13). *How to bleed a radiator.* Living - Your Home, DIY and Life by HomeServe. https://www.homeserve.com/uk/living/heating-and-cooling/how-to-bleed-a-radiator/

Food Standards Agency. (2021, March 19). *Best before and Use by Dates.* Food Standards Agency. https://www.food.gov.uk/safety-hygiene/best-before-and-use-by-dates

Foodviva.com. (n.d.). *Cooking Measurements and Conversions - How to Measure Food Ingredients.* Foodviva.com. https://foodviva.com/cooking-measurements-conversions/

Franco, M. G. (2019). *5 Skills for Making Friends as an Adult.* Www.psychologytoday.com. https://www.psychologytoday.com/gb/blog/platonic-love/201909/5-skills-making-friends-adult

GOV.UK. (2020). *How to rent a safe home.* GOV.UK. https://www.gov.uk/government/publications/how-to-rent-a-safe-home/how-to-rent-a-safe-home

Harvard Health Publishing. (2019). *5 of the best exercises you can ever do.*

Harvard Health. https://www.health.harvard.edu/staying-healthy/5-of-the-best-exercises-you-can-ever-do

hls_admin. (2020, September 3). *Know Your Toilet: How the Flapper Works and When to Replace It.* Adeedo. https://www.adeedo.com/know-your-toilet-how-the-flapper-works-and-when-to-replace-it/#:~:text=The%20toilet%20flapper%20is%20the

Holdefehr, K. (2020). *9 Basic Home Maintenance How-tos Everyone Should Know.* Real Simple. https://www.realsimple.com/home-organizing/home-improvement/maintenance-repairs/home-maintenance-basics

How Stuff Works. (2021, May 12). *How to Clean Your Dryer Vent.* HowStuffWorks. https://home.howstuffworks.com/home-improvement/home-diy/projects/dryer-vent-cleaning.htm

*How to Hang a Picture Without Nails : 3M United Kingdom & Ireland.* (2022). 3m.co.uk; MMM-ext. https://command.3m.co.uk/3M/en_GB/command-gb/how-to/how-to-hang-picture-without-nails/

InterNations. (n.d.). *Renting and Housing in the US: Everything You Need to Know.* InterNations. https://www.internations.org/usa-expats/guide/housing

Ivy Rehab Network. (2019, May 31). *Tech Neck - How Technology is Affecting Your Posture.* Ivy Rehab Network. https://www.ivyrehab.com/news/tech-neck-how-technology-is-affecting-your-posture/

KidsHealth. (2018). *How to Find Affordable Health Care (for Parents) - Nemours KidsHealth.* Kidshealth.org. https://kidshealth.org/en/parents/find-care.html

Leverette, M. M. (2021). *5 Laundry Products You Should Have on Your Shelf.* The Spruce. https://www.thespruce.com/laundry-products-everyone-needs-4150301

Maidforyou. (n.d.). *Home cleaning + Burning Calories = The Perfect Win-Win | MaidForYou.* Www.maidforyou.com.au. https://www.maidforyou.com.au/blog/calories-burned-cleaning-house/

Mana Medical Associates. (2017, May). *The Importance of Physical Fitness - Medical Associates of Northwest Arkansas.* Medical Associates of

Northwest Arkansas. https://www.mana.md/the-importance-of-physical-fitness/

Mark, L. A. (2021, March 23). *How to Remove Almost Every Type of Stain.* Reader's Digest. https://www.rd.com/article/how-to-remove-stains/

Metabolic Research Center. (n.d.). *HOW THE BODY USES CARBOHYDRATES, FATS AND PROTEINS.* Retrieved 21 October 2022, from https://www.emetabolic.com/locations/centers/siouxcity/blog/hormones-dna/how_the_body_uses_carbohydrates_fats_and_proteins/

Miller, G. (2021, May 13). *Dealing with Teen Emotions.* Psych Central. https://psychcentral.com/blog/techniques-for-teens-how-to-cope-with-your-emotions#donts

Molly Maid. (n.d.-a). *How to Clean a Refrigerator: Fridge Cleaning Tips from Molly Maid.* MOLLY MAID. https://www.mollymaid.com/cleaning-tips/kitchens/refrigerator-cleaning/

Molly Maid. (n.d.-b). *How to Clean a Showerhead | Tips for Clogged Showerheads.* MOLLY MAID. https://www.mollymaid.com/cleaning-tips/bathrooms/how-to-clean-a-showerhead/

Molly Maid. (n.d.-c). *How to Clean a Toilet | Best Way to Clean Toilet.* MOLLY MAID. https://www.mollymaid.com/cleaning-tips/bathrooms/how-to-clean-a-toilet/

Molly Maid. (n.d.-d). *How to Clean an Oven: Oven Cleaning Tips from Molly Maid.* MOLLY MAID. https://www.mollymaid.com/cleaning-tips/kitchens/oven-cleaning/

Nast, C. (2017, December 1). *How to Clean an Oven With Baking Soda in 10 Simple Steps.* Architectural Digest. https://www.architecturaldigest.com/story/how-to-clean-an-oven#:~:text=To%20make%20your%20DIY%20cleaner

Nationwide. (2020, September 4). *11 Efficient House Cleaning Tips.* Now from Nationwide ®. https://blog.nationwide.com/how-to-clean-house-fast/

NHS Choices. (2019a). *Cuts and grazes.* NHS. https://www.nhs.uk/conditions/cuts-and-grazes/

NHS Choices. (2019b). *Overview - Burns and scalds.* NHS. https://www.nhs.uk/conditions/burns-and-scalds/

NHS Choices. (2019c). *What should I keep in my first aid kit?* NHS. https://www.nhs.uk/common-health-questions/accidents-first-aid-and-treatments/what-should-i-keep-in-my-first-aid-kit/

NI Cyber Security Centre. (2021, August 5). *Secure Your Home.* NI Cyber Security Centre. https://www.nicybersecuritycentre.gov.uk/home-security

NUMBEO. (n.d.). *Price Rankings by Country of Apartment (1 bedroom) in City Centre (Rent Per Month).* Www.numbeo.com. https://www.numbeo.com/cost-of-living/country_price_rankings?itemId=26

OddHogg. (2020, September 8). *What Do You Have To Iron? Basic Ironing Tips.* OddHogg. https://oddhogg.com/ironing/

OutOfStress. (2021, February 23). *What Does It Mean to Know Your Worth? + 8 Reasons Why It's Important.* OutofStress.com. https://www.outofstress.com/know-your-worth/

Patelco Credit Union. (n.d.). *How to Stay on Top of Your Bills – Patelco Credit Union.* Www.patelco.org. Retrieved September 19, 2022, from https://www.patelco.org/financial-wellness/budgeting/stay-on-top-of-your-bills

Pepper, S. (2012, August 30). *Life Skills For Teenagers - Food Shopping.* Youth Workin' It. https://youthworkinit.com/life-skills-for-teenagers-food-shopping/

Perry, C. (2022, September 14). *How Much Do Movers Cost?* Forbes Home. https://www.forbes.com/home-improvement/moving-services/movers-and-packers-cost/

Picard, C. (2020, February 3). *Yes, You Can Fold Shirts Just Like Marie Kondo in Just 4 Simple Steps.* Good Housekeeping. https://www.goodhousekeeping.com/home/organizing/g2685/how-to-fold-clothes-to-save-space/

Plumb Time. (2020, July 5). *How to Clean Drains in Your Home (The Right Way!).* Plumber Columbia SC | Plumb Time Plumbing & Drain Services. https://www.plumbtimesc.com/how-to-clean-drains-the-right-way/

# BIBLIOGRAPHY | 177

PlumbNation. (2021). *How to Turn Off Your Water Supply to Your House.* PlumbNation. https://www.plumbnation.co.uk/blog/how-to-turn-off-your-water-supply-to-your-house/

Precise Plumbing & Electrical. (2019, July 24). *10 Tips For Unblocking Any Drain (DIY & Professional).* Precise Trade Services. https://preciseservices.com.au/10-tips-to-clear-any-blocked-drain/

Rooney, D. (2015, September 30). *The Basics: Essential Kitchen... Cook Smarts;* Cook Smarts. https://www.cooksmarts.com/cooking-guides/create-a-functional-kitchen/20-must-have-kitchen-tools/

Rupavate, S. (2014, February 11). *Top 11 reasons why you need to bathe everyday.* Www.thehealthsite.com. https://www.thehealthsite.com/diseases-conditions/top-11-reasons-you-need-to-bathe-everyday-sh214-119937/

Sarah Ever After. (2021, August 16). *Tidying vs Cleaning - Why The Difference Really Does Matter!* Sarah Ever After. https://saraheverafter.com/tidying-vs-cleaning/

Sharkey, L. (2019, November 19). *How Often Should You Actually Cut Your Hair?* Healthline. https://www.healthline.com/health/beauty-skin-care/how-often-should-you-cut-your-hair

Simon. (2019). *3 Key Tips to Never Get Locked Out Again.* Keyishoes. https://keyishoes.co.uk/3-key-tips-to-never-get-locked-out-again/

Smart Storage. (2019, June 25). *What Are the Benefits of Decluttering Your Home?* Smart Storage. https://www.smart-storage.co.uk/2019/06/the-benefits-of-a-decluttered-home/

SSE. (n.d.). *Boiler problems and solutions: help with common issues - SSE.* Sse.co.uk. https://sse.co.uk/help/home-services/common-boiler-problems

Team HomeServe USA. (2020). *How to Fix a Hole in the Wall like a Pro.* Www.homeserve.com. https://www.homeserve.com/en-us/blog/how-to/fix-hole-wall/

The Clean Haven. (2019, September 12). *Why It's Important To Regularly Clean Your Home.* The Clean Haven. https://thecleanhaven.com/why-its-important-to-regularly-clean-your-home/#:~:text=Cleaning%20every%20week%20will%20help

The Syndicate Post. (2016, November 19). *Positive Thinking Strategies for*

178 | BIBLIOGRAPHY

*Teens and Young Adults*. The Syndicate Post. https://medium.com/syndicate-post/positive-thinking-strategies-for-teens-and-young-adults-37465ced72c9

Torres, K. (2020, August 21). *5 Important Documents to Safely Store in Your Home in 2020*. SafeWise. https://www.safewise.com/blog/keep-important-documents-safe-home/

UHS. (n.d.). *What is open enrollment?* Www.uhc.com. https://www.uhc.com/understanding-health-insurance/open-enrollment

VAN DUYNE, A. (n.d.). *101 Culinary Terms Every Chef Knows - On the Line | Toast POS*. Pos.toasttab.com. https://pos.toasttab.com/blog/on-the-line/culinary-terms

Vann, M. R. (2013). *Skin Care for Teen Skin - Skin and Beauty Center - Everyday Health*. EverydayHealth.com. https://www.everydayhealth.com/skin-and-beauty/skin-care-for-teen-skin.aspx

Wallender, L. (2022). *How to Reset a Tripped Breaker*. The Spruce. https://www.thespruce.com/reset-a-tripped-breaker-4134193

Whirlpool. (n.d.). *How Often Should You Wash Your Clothes?*. Www.whirlpool.com. https://www.whirlpool.com/blog/washers-and-dryers/how-often-should-you-wash-your-clothes.html

Wikes. (n.d.). *How to Hang a Picture | Hanging Pictures | Wickes*. Www.wickes.co.uk. https://www.wickes.co.uk/how-to-guides/decorating/hang-a-picture

wikiHow Staff. (2019). *How to Turn Off Your Water Supply Quick and Easy*. In wikiHow. https://www.wikihow.com/Turn-Off-Your-Water-Supply-Quick-and-Easy

Witmer, D. (2019). *14 Essential Manners Every Teen Should Know*. Verywell Family. https://www.verywellfamily.com/manners-your-teen-should-use-and-how-to-teach-them-2608864

Young Minds. (n.d.). *Reaching Out For Help With Your Mental Health*. YoungMinds. https://www.youngminds.org.uk/young-person/your-guide-to-support/reaching-out-for-help/

Your Move. (n.d.). *First Time Renting Guide For Tenants*. Www.yourMove.co.uk. https://www.your-move.co.uk/rent/guides/guide-for-first-time-renters#

BIBLIOGRAPHY | 179

## Image References

3D Vector. (n.d.). *3D Key of house isolated on white.* Shutterstock. https://www.shutterstock.com/image-illustration/3d-key-house-isolated-on-white-567669820

Ablohina, V. (n.d.). *Kitchen conversions chart. Basic metric units of cooking measurements. Most commonly used volume measures, weight of liquids. Vector outline illustration.* Shutterstock. https://www.shutterstock.com/image-vector/kitchen-conversions-chart-basic-metric-units-1916778731

Alexander_P. (n.d.). *zombie hand out of the toilet sketch engraving vector illustration. T-shirt apparel print design. Scratch board imitation. Black and white hand drawn image.* Shutterstock. https://www.shutterstock.com/image-vector/zombie-hand-out-toilet-sketch-engraving-2147429141

AlexStreln. (n.d.). *Table setting, top view. Proper formal place setting guide. Dinner flatware.Plan for cutlery on table. Etiquette.Plate, fork, spoon, knife, wine glass.Utensils.Color flat vector illustration. Isolated.* Shutterstock. https://www.shutterstock.com/image-vector/table-setting-top-view-proper-formal-2142887675

Alka5051. (n.d.). *Hugging heart, hands holding heart, charity icon, love yourself, concept of volunteers. Vector illustration isolated on white background.* Shutterstock. https://www.shutterstock.com/image-vector/hugging-heart-hands-holding-charity-icon-1912536940

barrirret. (n.d.). *Love yourself quote. Self-care Single word. Modern calligraphy text love yourself Care. Design print for t shirt, pin label, badges, sticker, greeting card, banner. Vector illustration. ego.* Shutterstock. https://www.shutterstock.com/image-vector/love-yourself-quote-selfcare-single-word-1150989587

Colorcocktail. (n.d.). *Vector set of kitchen pots and pans with lids. Flat style.* Shutterstock. https://www.shutterstock.com/image-vector/vector-set-kitchen-pots-pans-lids-581580961

desdemona72 desdemona72. (n.d.). *keeping food safe by knowing what expiration dates mean.* Shutterstock. https://www.shutterstock.-

com/image-illustration/keeping-food-safe-by-knowing-what-1227674395

elenabsl. (n.d.). *Vitamin food sources and functions, rainbow wheel chart with food icons, healthy eating and healthcare concept.* Shutterstock. https://www.shutterstock.com/image-vector/vitamin-food-sources-functions-rainbow-wheel-424863853

fire_fly. (n.d.). *Herbs and spices set/ Housegrown herbs/ Culinary herbs in pots with labels/ Thyme, oregano, rosemary, basil, sage, parsley, mint sketches/ Hand drawn herbs and spices isolated/ Vector illustration.* Shutterstock. https://www.shutterstock.com/image-vector/herbs-spices-set-housegrown-culinary-pots-426410725

Fox Biz. (n.d.). *To buy list hand drawn doodle vector illustration, design element, icon, sticker. Isolated on white background. Easy to change color. To buy list element. Shopping time. Check list. Market, shop.* Shutterstock. https://www.shutterstock.com/image-vector/buy-list-hand-drawn-doodle-vector-1659343870

Gate, F. (n.d.). *The black and white button is sewn with a sewing needle and black thread to hold the two fabrics together in close-up. Photo for an article about sewing hobbies and sewing.* Shutterstock. https://www.shutterstock.com/image-photo/black-white-button-sewn-sewing-needle-1925164886

Gorda, L. (n.d.). *Kitchen utensils isolated on white photo-realistic vector illustration.* Shutterstock. https://www.shutterstock.com/image-vector/kitchen-utensils-isolated-on-white-photorealistic-373202557

GraphicsRF.com. (n.d.). *Illustration of a plate of omelet.* Shutterstock. https://www.shutterstock.com/image-vector/illustration-plate-omelet-249379954

Kamira. (n.d.). *Measuring cup containing water on a white background.* Shutterstock. https://www.shutterstock.com/image-photo/measuring-cup-containing-water-on-white-142760413

Katule. (n.d.). *Fitness Exercise Burpees.* Shutterstock. https://www.shutterstock.com/image-vector/fitness-exercise-burpees-626822438

KatyaNesterova. (n.d.). *Doodle vector hand drawn plumber, plunger for* *toilet and sink. Household supplies, cleaning service, clogging, vacuum cleaning, housekeeping, WC, hygiene. Design element for typography and digital.*https://www.shutterstock.com/image-vector/doodle-vector-hand-drawn-plumber-plunger-2106889478

LadadikArt. (n.d.-a). *Skin burn stages infographics and treatment. Thermal burns types, burning hands and medical care. Safety of fire, body skin first aid an injury recent vector poster.* Shutterstock. https://www.shutterstock.com/image-vector/skin-burn-stages-infographics-treatment-thermal-2166671537

LadadikArt. (n.d.-b). *Skin injury first aid for wound or burn. Bleeding from wounds, treatment and medical care. Self rescue tips and how stop blood, recent vector hospital info poster.* Shutterstock. https://www.shutterstock.com/image-vector/skin-injury-first-aid-wound-burn-2145531517

limeart. (n.d.). *Dental health icons. 8 tips healthy teeth editable stroke. Brush teeth regularly fluoride toothpaste floss once a day see a dentist regularly. Don't smoke mouthwash limit sugary foods drink more water.* Shutterstock. https://www.shutterstock.com/image-vector/dental-health-icons-8-tips-healthy-1831452685

Line_Design. (n.d.). *Stick figures. Together, every lock is opened and every problem is solved. Vector.* Shutterstock. https://www.shutterstock.com/image-vector/stick-figures-together-every-lock-opened-2033910572

lukpedclub. (n.d.). *measuring spoon, outline design icon.* Shutterstock. https://www.shutterstock.com/image-vector/measuring-spoon-outline-design-icon-650931064

Mack, R. (n.d.). *Illustration of a sausage and egg biscuit sandwich.* Shutterstock. https://www.shutterstock.com/image-vector/illustration-sausage-egg-biscuit-sandwich-196301507

medejaja. (n.d.). *Cooking chef information chart, illustrations demonstrating various kinds of knife cut chop techniques of fruit, vegtables.* Shutterstock. https://www.shutterstock.com/image-vector/cooking-chef-information-chart-illustrations-demonstrating-648116977

onot. (n.d.). *Colored hand sketch holding hands. Vector illustration.* Shutter-

## 182 | BIBLIOGRAPHY

stock. https://www.shutterstock.com/image-vector/colored-hand-sketch-holding-hands-vector-621426752

OurWork. (n.d.). *SWIPE RIGHT ICON, SLIDE TO RIGHT ICON.* Shutterstock. https://www.shutterstock.com/image-vector/swipe-right-icon-slide-1719113719

Panasovskyi, O. (n.d.). *Single brass radiator key. Vector outline icon.* Shutterstock. https://www.shutterstock.com/image-illustration/single-brass-radiator-key-vector-outline-1398693263

PattyK. (n.d.). *healthy eating for good health.* Shutterstock. https://www.shutterstock.com/image-vector/healthy-eating-good-health-363493640

Pavlyuk, A. (n.d.). *Summer salads. Vector watercolor illustration.* Shutterstock. https://www.shutterstock.com/image-vector/summer-salads-vector-watercolor-illustration-285741542

Pepermpron. (ca. 2022, September). *Choking first aid baby food CPR child step lodges blocking victim adult help abdomen kids conscious poster swallow back blows chest rescue breath care safety.* Shutterstock. https://www.shutterstock.com/image-vector/choking-first-aid-baby-food-cpr-2135380697

Poirier, F. (n.d.). *Illustration of cleaner icon on white background.* Shutterstock. https://www.shutterstock.com/image-vector/illustration-cleaner-icon-on-white-background-678454378

putra, L. (n.d.-a). *Man doing air squat in 2 steps in side view. Flat vector illustration isolated on white background.* Shutterstock. https://www.shutterstock.com/image-vector/man-doing-air-squat-2-steps-1830755837

putra, L. (n.d.-b). *Man doing Anjaneyasana or low lunge yoga pose. Flat vector illustration isolated on white background.* Shutterstock. https://www.shutterstock.com/image-vector/man-doing-anjaneyasana-low-lunge-yoga-1830754286

putra, L. (n.d.-c). *Woman doing Dumbbell push press exercise. Flat vector illustration isolated on white background.* Shutterstock. https://www.shutterstock.com/image-vector/woman-doing-dumbbell-push-press-exercise-1990675406

RDVector. (n.d.). *Scraper icon in line art style. Spatula vector illustration.*

Shutterstock. https://www.shutterstock.com/image-vector/scraper-icon-line-art-style-spatula-2116114937

Sasek, Z. (n.d.-a). *Cartoon stick figure drawing conceptual illustration of happy hungry man holding salt shaker and using pepper, salt or spice on food or soup.* Shutterstock. https://www.shutterstock.com/image-vector/cartoon-stick-figure-drawing-conceptual-illustration-1386446690

Sasek, Z. (n.d.-b). *Vector cartoon stick figure drawing conceptual illustration of aging process of human man, from baby to senior adult.* Shutterstock. https://www.shutterstock.com/image-vector/vector-cartoon-stick-figure-drawing-conceptual-1494108728

Sashkin. (n.d.). *First aid kit isolated.* Shutterstock. https://www.shutterstock.com/image-illustration/first-aid-kit-isolated-65624194

Semanche. (n.d.). *Stick man holding a rainbow in his hands. Doodle style. Vector illustration.* Shutterstock. https://www.shutterstock.com/image-vector/stick-man-holding-rainbow-his-hands-2070044894

Sergeeva, V. (n.d.-a). *Badge toilet glyph icon, vector cut monochrome badge for house plumbing promotion design.* Shutterstock. https://www.shutterstock.com/image-vector/badge-toilet-glyph-icon-vector-cut-1938817093

Sergeeva, V. (n.d.-b). *Hand drawn pancakes with strawberries and syrup. Decorative icon pancakes in an old style ink. Vector illustration of Pancakes on a plate.* Shutterstock. https://www.shutterstock.com/image-vector/hand-drawn-pancakes-strawberries-syrup-decorative-392311246

Shebeko. (n.d.). *chef cutting vegetables.* Shutterstock. https://www.shutterstock.com/image-photo/chef-cutting-vegetables-400683709

Shrivastava, A. (n.d.). *Circuit Breaker Icon, Overload, Short Circuit Protector Switch Vector Art Illustration.* Shutterstock. https://www.shutterstock.com/image-vector/circuit-breaker-icon-overload-short-protector-1715194858

SimpleEPS. (n.d.). *Vector illustration of types of kitchen knives: chefâ??s, meat cleaver, small bread, carving, banning, paring, steak, fork, bread.* Shutterstock. https://www.shutterstock.com/image-vector/vector-illustration-types-kitchen-knives-meat-392287537

## 184 | BIBLIOGRAPHY

solar22. (n.d.). *Step instruction for push up of woman. Cartoon illustration about work out.* Shutterstock. https://www.shutterstock.com/image-vector/step-instruction-push-woman-cartoon-illustration-454190938

stick-figures.com. (n.d.). *Smiling Stickman Doing Weight lifting.* Shutterstock. https://www.shutterstock.com/image-vector/smiling-stickman-doing-weight-lifting-1540249622

Toltemara. (n.d.). *Clothing Organization Steps. Vector Illustration with a Big Messy Pile of Useless, Old, Cheap, and Oumoded Cothes and several boxes to organize it properly.* Shutterstock. https://www.shutterstock.com/image-vector/clothing-organization-steps-vector-illustration-big-1351511876

Trueffelpix. (n.d.-a). *Optimism is a mental attitude or world view that interprets situations and events as being best.* Shutterstock. https://www.shutterstock.com/image-vector/optimism-mental-attitude-world-view-that-186473060

Trueffelpix. (n.d.-b). *Team carrying boxes and furniture into a moving van.* Shutterstock. https://www.shutterstock.com/image-vector/team-carrying-boxes-furniture-into-moving-602586029

Ustiugova, D. (n.d.). *Delicious grilled salmon fish fillet with lemon, rosemary and spicies. Watercolor hand drawn illustration, isolated on white background.* Shutterstock. https://www.shutterstock.com/image-illustration/delicious-grilled-salmon-fish-fillet-lemon-1287107542

vector_ann. (n.d.). *Watercolor mixed berries smoothie composition in a jar with straw on white background. Watercolour healthy food illustration.* Shutterstock. https://www.shutterstock.com/image-illustration/watercolor-mixed-berries-smoothie-composition-jar-1891476517

Viktoriia_P. (n.d.). *Preservation, set. Two jars of cucumbers and tomatoes. Sketch scratch board imitation.* Shutterstock. https://www.shutterstock.com/image-vector/preservation-set-two-jars-cucumbers-tomatoes-1810453366

Yulia, R. (n.d.). *Vector graphics diagram of vertical folding of things.* Shutterstock. https://www.shutterstock.com/image-vector/vector-graphics-diagram-vertical-folding-things-1807310632

YummyBuum. (n.d.). *Laundry icons. Care clothes instructions on labels, machine or hand washing signs. Water, ironing and drying temperature symbols collection, textile and fabric types. Vector line items isolated set.* Shutterstock. https://www.shutterstock.com/image-vector/laundry-icons-care-clothes-instructions-on-1892432443

Printed in Great Britain
by Amazon